British Heart Fou...

York.   Sunday ...

MW00668653

GAME PLAN

A MODERN WOMAN'S SURVIVAL KIT

GAME PLAN
A MODERN WOMAN'S SURVIVAL KIT

KATE O'MARA

SIDGWICK & JACKSON LIMITED
LONDON

First published in Great Britain in 1990 by
Sidgwick & Jackson Ltd
1 Tavistock Chambers, Bloomsbury Way
London WC1A 2SG

ISBN 0 283 06057 3

Typeset by Hewer Text, Edinburgh
Printed by Mackays of Chatham Ltd, Kent.

ACKNOWLEDGEMENTS

My grateful thanks to:

Christine Royalle for her tireless efforts, and without whose help this book would not have been written.

The various actors and actresses mentioned in the book, some of whom have been consulted and the rest of whom I trust will not mind too much.

CONTENTS

INTRODUCTION

In 1985, at the age of forty-six, I went to Hollywood. Two years later I founded my own theatre company. Both were high points in a life and a career that has seen its up and downs. I am also a mother – not perhaps the best in the world, but I now have a grown-up son of whom I am very proud. And underpinning it all have been innumerable stormy and passionate relationships with men – a species about whom I feel eternally ambivalent. Something tells me they are all immature boys, and they cause one endless emotional torment, yet I cannot live my life without them.

But this book was never intended to be an autobiography. Indeed readers may find there are some areas which I do not touch on at all, or about which I have given very little detail. That is my privilege; for I am, despite the attempts of some sections of the press to make it seem otherwise, a very private person. One thing that this book most certainly will reveal is the real me, rather than the on-stage rich-bitch persona that some people mistakenly believe is also the off-stage Kate O'Mara. And that real KOM is someone who takes a strong and very personal moral stance about some of the burning issues of the late twentieth century.

I feel my life has been somewhat less planned and organised than the book's title would suggest – I have developed a survival kit as a result of it all, rather than starting out with a calculated game plan. Indeed I like to take life as it comes, grasping the opportunities of the moment in case tomorrow never comes. So what this book is really aimed at is to show how I have survived it all. Often I've just managed to come out on top.

Finally, a word of warning. This book is not for the faint-hearted. It pulls no punches. There are no holds barred. It is dedicated to today's new woman – the woman who is quite capable of indulging in hitherto exclusively masculine be-haviour and yet is not afraid to express her own femininity.

1

Born to Tread
the Boards

My earliest memories are of being backstage in a world of mystery and magic, for I had the good fortune to be born into a theatrical family. When I was a child my father was away in the RAF and my mother was often on tour. I spent a great deal of time with my grandparents, who managed theatres. As they frequently didn't know what to do with me, I got plonked into one of the boxes in the theatre and sat in resplendent solitude watching show after show, week after week. Sometimes I would see the same show six or seven times. I thought it was wonderful.

I also spent a great deal of my time in dressing rooms waiting for my mother to come off stage, and sometimes I was allowed into the wings where I would gaze in awe and wonder at beautiful men waiting to go on stage. They were beautiful, of course, because in those days even in a straight theatre they wore a great deal of make-up, particularly on their eyes. I have had a penchant for men in eye make-up ever since!

Shakespeare came early into my life, although I did not recognise him. Whenever as a little girl I crossed the road with my mother, she would say, 'Give me your hand, Bassanio'. Until I read *The Merchant of Venice* at the age of about ten, I was under the impression that 'Bassanio' was a term of endearment. Imagine my surprise when I discovered it to be the opening lines of Antonio's farewell speech to his friend!

Mealtimes in my grandparents' eccentric seaside house in Brighton were accompanied by constant talk of box office takings and the financial problems of theatre management. This early experience has stood me in good stead since starting my own theatre company. By that I mean that these problems do not worry me unduly; they are familiar to me.

It was inevitable that I would become an actress, and to me inevitable that I should have my own theatre company – simply a matter of going into the family business. Actors who have no theatrical connections at all fascinate me. I always admire their initiative and tenacity in going into a profession which in many cases has been not only foreign to them, completely unknown territory, but also often thoroughly disapproved by their families. I always ask them what made them think of becoming actors, how they got the idea; it is something which to me has been part of my life ever since I can remember, but to them it must once have seemed extraordinary indeed. Often I find it is the cinema that has inspired them, particularly actors of my own generation brought up on post-war escapist 1950s' movies. They too felt a longing to be part of that wonderful make-believe world.

But from my early close contact with the profession I knew that acting involved hard graft as well as dreams. There have been times when I have been living off peanut butter sand-

2

wiches, and then two days later found myself in the back of a Rolls Royce being whisked off to an expensive lunch at a fashionable eating place. One moment I have been sitting in jeans and tee-shirts in a cold, grubby rehearsal room, and the next found myself in the South of France sitting by a swimming pool surrounded by paparazzi and international stars. But the uncertainty is what I like. One of the great things about this profession is that you never know what's going to happen next. There's no chance of getting bored. And it always seems to turn out that when you're at your lowest ebb, and there is absolutely no money at all, the most amazing job turns up which completely alters your lifestyle, even if it's only for two or three months.

One of the really marvellous things about my profession is that it is a great social leveller. There are no barriers of class, sex, colour or creed. You are judged only on your ability. I have found actors, both male and female, to be among the most compassionate, gentle, witty, charming, intelligent and generous people I have ever met.

But along with all this stimulus and companionship go the hard times when you're desperate for a job. Auditions teach you a lot about the profession, and about life in general. I remember being one of three hundred girls trying to get one part in the West End. I got recalled five times. As the numbers dwindled my hopes rose. The last twenty, the last twelve, the last six and finally the last two. It was between myself and another actress. But in the event, neither of us got it. An actress they had never seen before suddenly walked in on the off-chance, and got the part. It was a great lesson in survival.

I auditioned three years running for one particular theatrical season and, although it was obvious that the manager liked me – otherwise presumably he wouldn't have asked me back – his directors simply did not take to me. When I didn't get in for the third time, I was devastated as I had my heart set on joining the company. Nineteen years later I was asked to join the company as the star for the season, and went back to do a further two seasons for them. So it came full circle and I did the three seasons that I should have done before. As my mother would say, 'You see, God is good to little actresses.' This was by way of giving me encouragement for the future, to have faith in myself and my own ability.

She was full of theatrical wisdom, and gave me two very sound pieces of advice. 'Now don't forget dear,' she told me, 'a nice clean performance, and plenty of attack.' Certainly a clean performance is very desirable; by that she meant clarity of thought, economy of movement and perfect diction. By attack I think she meant energy. I believe energy is all-important – it is what makes an actor watchable. It matters not whether it is outward-going or contained: energy is of the essence. The other piece of advice from my mother – every bit as important in its way – was 'Never wear white shoes on stage!' She was absolutely right, because white shoes makes one's feet look enormous. If I see an actress wearing white shoes on stage I am completely riveted by her feet and can look at nothing else. They gleam and catch the light, and it is very difficult to tear your eyes away to look at her face.

Sometimes I feel I would have benefited from my mother's insight and experience, for I am afraid that my judgement is not always on the ball when choosing scripts. I am inclined to go for those that appeal to me and my taste, rather than considering what the public would prefer to see. I have made a couple of fairly big mistakes in this way. I am not a typical member of an audience, and I tend to forget this when making a decision. One play, however, that I was convinced would be a riot was *Light Up the Sky*, which turned out to be a terrific success.

One can never plan anything in this profession, and it is often when one is at one's lowest ebb that a glorious job turns up. In this instance my career was in the doldrums, my box office appeal was zilch, and I was seriously considering giving up acting all together. I was in the middle of composing a letter to send round to various theatres to ask them if they would consider me as a potential Assistant Director, when two things happened. I was asked to test for *The Colbys* and I was sent a brilliant script by Moss Hart. I tested for *The Colbys* on the Thursday, and received the script for the play on the Friday. After months of being out of work and near-suicidal, I got both jobs! Not *The Colbys*, but the studio decided I was perfect to play Joan Collins's sister in *Dynasty*. As I had already started rehearsals for *Light Up the Sky*, I was unable to accept the Hollywood offer; at first this was a severe disappointment to me, because at that time Joan Collins was the biggest international star around and to play her sister was quite a coup. Fortunately the studio decided to wait for me, and write me into the series after I had finished the West End run of the play.

I had first seen Joan at Pinewood Studios in 1967, where we were both making movies. I remember sitting in the studio restaurant and observing her at the next table. I couldn't take my eyes off her! I thought her the most beautiful woman I had ever seen. The other day I was having lunch with her in a restaurant in Belgravia and I have to say I have not changed my opinion. Joan has the most beautiful complexion and perfect features. She has a wicked sense of humour, a sparkling personality and a ready wit, and is a delight to be with socially and highly professional at work – I enjoyed doing my scenes with her more than anything. She is a consummate film actress and I learned a lot from her. Although *Dynasty* itself was an achievement, to me it was a means to an even greater achievement. There is no doubt that without that series I would never have been able to start my theatre company, which has proved to be the most satisfying venture of my entire life so far. Our aim is to bring theatre of a high quality to as many people as possible. I know it is true that many people come to see me simply because of my

TV appearances, but I like to think that they have an experience they have not hitherto enjoyed – seeing an energetic production of a well-loved classic. I have always thought it would be quite nice to be the first inter-terrestrial classical theatre company, but I shall be content if one day we manage to have our very own theatre. Films may come and go, television may come and go, but live theatre has been around since time immemorial and will continue to be so until the end of the world.

Something quite miraculous happens when the curtain goes up in a darkened theatre; for me it surpasses anything that happens in a movie house. I suppose it is because it is live. The greatest feeling when on stage is to be relaxed enough to believe moment by moment everything that is happening, to live every second of the drama that one is telling.

The ghastly repetition of film-making, the tedium of constantly having to recapture the live moment and make it fresh every time, is for me soul-destroying. I enormously admire accomplished film actors. God knows how they do it – it is not for me. I have made several movies in my time and hardly ever enjoyed myself. The only satisfaction to be gained is the hope that one has acquitted oneself in a technically-competent manner. The same applies to television: one is so much at the mercy of the technicalities of the medium that for me the artistic inspiration is killed. It is the spontaneous improvisatory danger of live theatre that is my life blood.

The public seems to be fascinated by one particular aspect of live theatre: one is continually being asked how one remembers one's lines. Some actors find this part of the job very easy, some very difficult. I confess I rather enjoy the process of committing page upon page of dialogue to memory. I regard it as a challenge and it is great mental exercise. If I am doing a very large part, I invariably learn the biggest speeches first. If there is a huge speech, that is the one I will start with. This is in order to give me a feeling of security, so that instead of thinking as I approach a particularly large chunk, 'Oh, my God – that big speech is coming up', I think, 'Oh, great, I know this bit.'

I much prefer playing large parts – I find them much easier. I have the chance to relax into them and get into the swing of things, and I can dictate the pace of the play. The hardest parts in the world to play are small parts or supporting roles, and in particular small flashy parts. To have to wait for hours and then bound on to the stage and be utterly brilliant and bound off again is nerve-racking. The tension builds up in an alarming way, no matter how hard one tries to overcome it. Whereas if one is on stage for most of the performance, the space begins to feel like home and one becomes more and more confident. It is a great feeling.

Having power over an audience is an extraordinary experience: making them laugh or cry, or just be utterly silent and stop coughing, is heady stuff indeed. Occasionally, if there is someone in the audience with a bad cough, I will repeat lines that have been drowned out. This is not easy in Shakespeare as it can destroy the rhythm of the speech, but sometimes it is essential if the plot is to be understood by the rest of the audience. Another thing that the public always wants to know about is one's feelings for one's leading man. It is inevitable, I suppose, that one falls in love a little bit with the hero of the piece, particularly if one is playing opposite him. One has, after all, to convince the audience and, hopefully, one's fellow actors that the romance is real, and to do this one has to believe it a little oneself. I have a dreadful tendency to fall for my leading men, particularly if it is a wonderful play enjoying a long run. But of course it is very dangerous and one should not really allow oneself the indulgence, especially if there is mutual attraction. I suspect that this may be one of the reasons that so many show business marriages founder.

However, I have to say that I am seldom turned on by physical contact with my leading actor. There seems to be some sort of psychological safety valve that goes into operation when one has to kiss or pretend to make love on stage or in front of the cameras. I don't know quite which is the hardest to do. On camera one is seen in such close-up that one has to simulate something approaching the genuine article, whereas on stage, because one is seen from a distance, one can pretend more. But because it is live and therefore apparently happening for real it is much easier, I think, to get carried away in the theatre.

I never worry about nude scenes; I have had to do them on stage and on camera, and they now bother me not at all. They became fashionable in the sixties, which was my heyday, and one became very blasé about them. This also applies to bath scenes, bed scenes and any other forms of entertainment which require complete lack of inhibition. I don't think I have any inhibitions left. The theatre certainly knocks that out of one, as does having a baby. In both cases, one is being observed by countless people, often of the opposite sex, in the most intimate and revealing positions. I simply close my mind to the whole thing, pretend it is not happening and get on with it. I also employ this method when having to make personal public appearances. I loathe my public image so much that it distresses me to have to appear in that role. But more of that later.

The theatre is a small world and one can get very close to one's fellow players, especially during the run of a stage play. It breeds a kind of camaraderie that can result in horseplay and practical jokes. I was the unwitting instrument of one such piece of tomfoolery that nearly went too far. At the time I felt I was being highly unprofessional; however, the episode did cause a great deal of amusement.

Wyndham's Theatre is next door to the New Theatre – so close, in fact, that there is an interconnecting bridge from one to the other. I was appearing in Iris Murdoch and James Saunders's *The Italian Girl* at Wyndham's, and was also persuaded to make an unscheduled appearance in the wings of its neighbouring theatre.

The play at The New was John Osborne's *Hotel in Amsterdam*. At a certain moment the star, Paul Scofield, had to turn upstage right and glance towards the wings where his stage wife was supposedly packing. At various matinee performances the cast had managed to produce some sort of side-show to entertain Mr Scofield when he glanced off stage, in the hope of sabotaging his performance for the next few moments. They had tried pulling ghastly faces, wearing masks and doing sundry obscene things. I think I am right in saying that this particular matinee was the final one in the run of the play and the cast felt obliged to surpass themselves in their ingenuity.

In *The Italian Girl* I was playing a strange Murdochean character, a sort of Russian witch who was installed in the household as the mistress. Except that she didn't live in the house but in a sort of strange shed or hut somewhere in the garden. I was dressed fairly scantily, in a very torn Victorian nightdress which was off one shoulder, ripped up to the thigh and hanging off the other shoulder. It was quite a fetching garment. The plan was that I was to appear in the wings at the crucial moment, holding up a placard with some words written on it that were pertinent to the action and would hopefully reduce the great actor to convulsions. But the cast decided that for me to be in my nightdress, or rather half out of my nightdress, was not enough. Oh no, I was to be nude.

So in the middle of a matinee performance of *The Italian Girl*, Timothy West guided me across the interconnecting bridge between the two theatres and down the backstage stairs into the wings of the New Theatre where *Hotel in Amsterdam* was in progress. You may wonder how we managed to do this. Well, both Tim and I had a longish wait between entrances at the other theatre; he had gauged it to the very second and reckoned that we would have enough time for me to make this guest appearance.

I arrived in the wings to find the remainder of the *Hotel* cast in

9

an advanced state of anticipation and excitement. I was given the placard and told to kneel on the floor in the appropriate entrance. I obediently did this, and then took my nightdress off. As I had a nude scene with Richard Pasco in my own play, this did not worry me at all. So there I knelt with nothing on, holding up this placard ready for the moment when Paul Scofield would glance into the wings. On stage with Paul was David Burke. Off stage in the wings with me were Timothy West, Isobel Dean, Judy Parfitt and Joss Ackland. They were apoplectic with barely concealed mirth – I remember them stuffing handkerchiefs into their mouths to try to stop themselves laughing aloud.

When the moment arrived, Paul wandered upstage to the exit where I was stationed. He glanced into the wings and stopped dead in his tracks. He froze, in fact. I dutifully held up my placard. He wandered away slightly downstage, and then came back for a second look, plainly not having been able to believe his eyes. He stared in amazement at my completely naked body, attempted to read the placard, make a strange noise in his throat and waved in a vague manner. The rest of the cast were crying with laughter, clutching various parts of their anatomy and generally having a wonderful time. Paul turned away and wandered downstage again. Of course it was impossible for us to see what was happening on stage – which was precisely nothing. There was total and absolute silence. It went on for what seemed hours. Finally, Paul made a noise rather like a strangulated turkey and then stopped again. David Burke came in with his line, which was almost unintelligible as it was consumed with laughter. Another silence ensued. I was appalled, as I realised I had managed to bring the play to a complete standstill!

I could hear David Burke trying to rescue the situation in a voice shaking with laughter, and Paul Scofield attempting to speak to no avail. At this juncture, Tim West suddenly realised that we had a scene coming up in the adjoining theatre and grabbed hold of me to take me back. Hastily covering myself, I left a scene of utter chaos and ruin behind me and scampered off to Wyndham's just in time to go on for my next scene with Tim. We found our own cast waiting to hear what had happened and they doubled up with laughter as we described the scene. By this time I had got over my nerves and was beginning to see the funny side of it myself.

However, when I went home that night and described the whole scene to the man who was then my husband, he was not amused and said I should be ashamed of myself for doing something so unprofessional. Well, maybe I should. It is, I think, the only time I have stopped the show, literally.

Of course the great thing about live theatre is that it is precisely what it is. Live. Anything can happen, and frequently does. In a production of *The Rivals*, with the Welsh Theatre Company, I actually saved two of the actors' lives. I don't think they have ever fully appreciated this. It happened in the last act of the play. The young lovers, Falkland and Julia, were sitting in a sort of arbour, engaged in a rather charming love scene. I was standing in the downstage left wing area watching this scene with much enjoyment, as they were both rather good.

Suddenly, to my horror, I noticed that the arbour was starting to lean in a rather alarming way, and that it was gradually falling towards them. I gazed in fascination for a couple of seconds and then rushed round to see what had happened. The offending flat had come free of its moorings. I grabbed the brace which was supposed to be attached to a stage weight that was holding it up, and endeavoured to haul it back up again. This of course was impossible, as it was a huge flat and I'm only a little person. There was not a stage hand in sight, or any other actor for that matter. So there I stood, hanging on for grim life to this flat which I was just about managing to keep in a status quo. I could hear the cue for my entrance getting nearer and nearer. Desperately I gazed wildly around for assistance, and thankfully saw someone, an assistant stage manager, I think, in the dim light passing me. I hissed at him to help me. It seemed to take him ages to understand the full drama of the situation, but finally he came to my rescue.

By this time my entrance cue had come and gone and the two lovers were frantically busking on stage. Dialogue bearing not too much resemblance to Sheridan was being uttered in a somewhat strained, unnatural manner on stage as they valiantly struggled to keep the audience amused while they waited for me to appear. I handed over the flat to the ASM, and with my heart pounding picked up my skirts and rushed round to the door where I should have made my entrance. I hurled myself on stage, breathless with terror. My entrance was met by two extremely cross lovers who glared at me furiously for subjecting them to this unnecessary torment.

I don't think they really believed me when I explained to them afterwards that I, and I alone, was responsible for saving their lives. The Julia in question was the lovely actress Pamela Miles, who is now married to Tim Piggott-Smith. If she should ever read this, I would be only too happy to accept a small potted plant by way of expressing her gratitude for my heroism!

In 1982 I toured Yugoslavia with a play called *Duet for One*, a marvellous piece of theatre about a virtuoso violinist who is stricken with multiple sclerosis. There are only two characters in the show. Philip Madoc, a marvellous actor, played the psychiatrist. Apart from being a smashing actor, Philip can also speak every language known to man, or indeed woman, and therefore proved invaluable since he acted as our interpreter wherever we went. However, there's not a lot anyone can do about the situation that arose on our first night in Skopje.

A few years before the town had suffered a massive earthquake; the theatre we were playing in had not been used for some time, and had never seen an English theatre company before. The place was packed to the rafters. They had brought their aunts, uncles, grandparents, children and babies to see this show, not a word of which could they possibly understand, and which contained very little action although obviously a great deal of emotion. Philip and I knew we had quite a task ahead of us, but I have a firm belief that good acting transcends all language barriers. This I have found to be true on many occasions, most memorably when I was in Finland and witnessed the leading Finnish actress, Kuliki Forsell, give a most moving performance of two one-woman plays by the Spanish dramatist Lorca. I did not understand a word, and yet I understood everything.

I went on stage that night in Yugoslavia in my wheelchair full of apprehension, because a lot of people had paid a lot of money to see me and I didn't want to let them down, and yet I could not see how they could possibly understand or enjoy the play. The part consists of huge monologues, and it requires concentration of a high order to get through them. Suddenly I became aware of a great deal of clicking and flashing coming from one of the side boxes. As it was essential that I communicate my feelings to the audience – not being able to communicate through my words – this grew intolerable. I glanced over to the box and saw a crowd of photographers taking pictures of me whilst I was trying to create an atmosphere for the audience. I became absolutely incensed. I continued, however, but the moment I came off stage after the first scene I stated categorically that I would not go on again unless they were removed. I think it is the only time in my life that I have ever been able to get photographers moved. They left, and the show continued.

I was in the middle of a very dramatic scene when suddenly downstage a hatch popped open and a head appeared through the stage floor. I could hardly believe my eyes. It stayed there watching me. I glared at it. It continued to watch with great interest. I continued with the next speech, glaring all the while at the offending head. I manoeuvred the electric wheelchair downstage so that I was immediately beside him. Not knowing the Yugoslavian for 'Fuck off', I told him in English. He smiled happily at me and continued to gaze at me. I made an angry gesture with my hand for him to remove himself, but he just stayed there. I continued with the scene and drove the wheelchair up centre stage. I then turned round, rather in the manner of a bull about to charge a toreador. The head was still there, gazing happily at the scene, so I charged him. He could see the look in my eyes, and I could see the look of dawning horror in his as he realised I was attempting to decapitate him. He disappeared down his little hole very quickly indeed.

The scene continued and I started to get the audience back, and I like to think that they were enjoying themselves. I was just in the middle of a really big emotional bit, when to my utter disbelief the hatch popped up again and the disembodied head reappeared. I turned around on him basilisk-like, and he could see that I meant business. This time I didn't have to charge – he disappeared hastily.

There were many other distractions of this nature – children running around with ice-creams, babies yelling, and people talking to each other trying to understand what it was all about. But we received a rapturous ovation at the final curtain and I really believe the audience understood and enjoyed the evening. I think this is probably the nearest I have ever been to appearing in what must be very similar to the conditions in the Elizabethan theatre.

That might be considered an unusual role for me to be playing, for I have frequently found myself type-cast as a glamorous creature. Given the role models with which I identified when I was young, this is perhaps hardly surprising. As a girl I never had pin-ups of male singers or film stars on my bedroom walls: Elvis Presley or Pat Boone or Fernando Lamas were nowhere to be seen. However, I did have one entire wall approximately fifteen feet long by ten feet deep covered in a montage of glamorous female pin-ups. Everyone from Sophia Loren, Corinne Calvet, Jane Russell, Rita Hayworth, Susan Hayward, Lana Turner, Arlene Dahl, Rhonda Fleming, Elizabeth Taylor, Marilyn Monroe – you name them, they were there. The entire wall was covered with beautiful women in glorious technicolour. Apart from my proper life as a classical actress, I also manage to appear in the odd television drama. Usually as a tough glamorous business woman. I have managed to combine these two aspects of my career successfully now for over 30 years. I am quite calculating about it. In the theatre I have played any number of different types of women but on television and in the days when I used to make movies, the women I played were invariably sexy and exotic and glamorous.

The public always imagines that the world of the movies is glamorous and exciting. There are moments when it becomes so, but on the whole it is a very repetitive job, with long hours and a great deal of tension and pressure, which I have already touched on when talking about why I prefer working in the theatre. One meets many amusing and entertaining people, but on an actual movie set one has to be forever ready to leap up and perform for the cameras. One's concentration must be absolute, and one cannot afford to divert one's thoughts too much.

This, of course, is after one has actually got the job. There is – or rather was – an unpleasant factor in this particular branch of the profession which was prevalent during the sixties and early seventies. It was well known before that as well, but my film career was at its height during these years. I refer, of course, to the casting couch. I know that people think it is just part of the Hollywood myth; but sadly there really was a breed of producer and director who abused their power in this way.

I was fortunate enough to get my first big movie break in a film called *Great Catherine* and was not subjected to the embarrass-ment and indignity of casting couch auditioning. I was consi-dered for this film because I had appeared in stage productions of the classics, and the film was an adaptation of a play by Bernard Shaw. The star was Peter O'Toole and the producer was Jules Buck. I was sent to meet Peter for an initial interview. We got on famously, and I was then requested to audition for him. At the time I was working with Roger Moore; we were filming an episode of *The Saint*, in which I was playing the part of an Italian racing driver.

A car was sent to pick me up after we had finished shooting one evening and drove me to Eaton Place. Tired and terrified, I read the part of Varinka whilst O'Toole played all the other parts – brilliantly, of course. He was at the height of his fame, and I had thought him quite wonderful in *Lawrence of Arabia*. The result of this audition seems to have been a foregone conclusion, as champagne was already flowing.

That was in the days when I used to drink – though not very much. I was persuaded to take a couple of glasses, so I dread to think what sort of reading I gave; it probably broke down my inhibition, at any rate. At one point Peter had to come in shouting and he asked me to top him in volume. This was no easy matter – he has an enormous voice, and I was only twenty-six at the time and my vocal range had not attained the power that it has today. However, I did my best and yelled. I was required to read virtually the whole part and improvise with Peter. Jules was watching, and the director was also present.

Just when I thought we had finished, Peter suddenly pointed to a scene with the Empress Catherine in which I had quite a large speech. He said that he wanted me to decide which part of the speech was directed at Catherine and which not, and then reverse them. By this time, the combination of champagne and exhaustion – I had, after all, been up at the crack of dawn and filming all day – was making the script dance in front of my eyes. I plunged in and made a completely arbitrary choice, which turned out to be the right one. I saw them all glance at each other with nods of approval. I was then sent out of the room while they had a chat about me.

I went to the loo and hovered around, trying to repair my somewhat flushed face and wondering how long I should give them. Eventually I went into the kitchen and pottered about. I was then summoned into the living room where Peter took me by the shoulders and kissed me on the forehead, saying, 'We think you can do it.' I was driven home and fell into bed in a state of emotional and physical collapse. I had to be up early next morning for more filming, but when I arrived at the studio I found that I had completely lost my voice.

I had to endure a great deal of ribbing from Roger Moore. Working with Roger is really one of the pleasant things in life. He is always affable, entertaining, amusing, charming – a very intelligent, witty man who never loses his rag and is always utterly professional. I have been cast opposite him about half a dozen times in my career and have always known that I was going to have a good time. On this occasion I was teased unmercifully when at lunchtime it was confirmed that I had got the part. He insisted on calling me alternately Kate O'Stara and Starlet O'Mara!

The manner in which I got the part in *Great Catherine* is the proper way to get work: by being seen in something, recommended to someone, auditioning or reading for certain people, and being offered the job. In other words, one has proved oneself. Unfortunately, there are many other incidents in my career which have not been so happy.

I remember on one occasion being asked to meet a producer for a part in a film which was to star Elvis Presley. It was a scorching hot August day in the late sixties – 1967 or 1968 – the era of the micro-skirt, which was even tinier than the mini. For this interview I wore what was then regulation dress – my tiny pink mini-skirt or, as the men used to call them, pussy pelmet – a minute tight top and a great deal of hair and eye make-up.

17

I went up to the producer's suite at one of the big London hotels and was ushered in to see a very charming American. He gave me a script to look at and disappeared into an adjoining room. I started to read the scenes he had indicated and knew that I was quite capable of playing either of the two girls. When he re-emerged, he was in a towelling dressing gown. All the alarm bells in my head started ringing furiously. Admittedly it was a very hot day, and for all I know he might have just taken a shower; but the signs did not look good.

He sat beside me and read the part that Elvis was to play whilst I read one of the girl's parts. He seemed impressed with my reading and said that he thought I was in with a good chance. Then he asked me to stand up so that he could see my figure. This was not unusual – one was used to the Americans demanding this sort of parade, for looks were, and still are for all I know, of the essence to them. I obliged and stood before him. He asked me to turn round so that I had my back to him, and as I did so he reached forward, put his hand up my skirt and pulled down my knickers to my ankles.

I whipped round in disbelief, hurled the script at him, screaming obscenities the whiles, and endeavoured to make a dignified exit whilst simultaneously trying to pull my knickers up. I got to the door, turned round and screamed more abuse at him, and then, clutching my knickers, which by now I had managed to get up to my knees, slammed the door and raced down the corridor to the lift. As I was beating this hasty retreat I could hear him calling after me in a rather plaintive voice: 'Katie, Katie, what did I do?'

I got down to the hotel lobby and phoned my then agent, who seemed to be under the impression that I had handled the whole thing rather badly. By this time I was sobbing with the humiliation of the whole episode. I can only assume from this particular producer's attitude that he was used to aspiring young film actresses being rather more compliant.

In those days, being highly impoverished, I was not able to afford a car – indeed there were occasions when one couldn't afford to eat. But one certainly didn't have one's own transport. So occasionally, after a long day's shooting, if the studio hadn't provided a car one had to take a cab which one could ill afford or walk miles to the nearest tube station, or, worse still, wait in the dark for a bus that might or might not appear. Thus it came about that I accepted a life from a television studio boss after making an episode of some popular TV series. I found myself in the back of a chauffeur-driven car winging its way to central London. This was a tremendous relief, as I knew I should get home quickly and safely – or so I thought.

I was appalled when this particular man put his hand rather high up on my thigh and started making faintly obscene suggestions to me, in full hearing of the chauffeur. I replied rather haughtily that I was not that type of girl, that I didn't do such things with people I didn't know. He replied that in that case I was a very silly little girl and would never get on in the business. I replied heatedly that I most certainly would and didn't need to reduce myself to a level of a prostitute to do so. I could see the chauffeur's ears twitching animatedly whilst the rest of him remained as impassive as he could make himself. Thank God for his presence, as I managed to get home safely. But it is interesting that I have never worked for that particular studio again.

I have another sad tale of discrimination to relate. I had been offered a part by another television studio in an episode of something or other, and the head of casting asked me to accompany him to the first night of a musical. My agent thought this was a very good idea, and so, suitably dolled up, I went to the theatre. It was a very pleasant evening; we had drinks in the interval, and he offered to take me for supper afterwards. I declined, saying I needed to get home to relieve the babysitter. So he said he would drive me home. But just before we got there he stopped the car and made an impassioned pass at me. I was completely taken aback and resisted. He made it clear that it was in my interests to comply. I told him to fuck off.

That episode happened over twenty-five years ago and that casting director, who I know likes my work, has never cast me in anything since. Indeed there was one occasion when the director of a TV programme asked him to check my availability; he pretended to do so and told the director that I was unavailable. Unfortunately for him, the director checked with my agent who told him that I *was* free, so I got the part over his head. This gave me a certain amount of satisfaction.

I have never come across this sort of problem in the theatre; it would appear that this attitude goes with that sector of the business in which a great deal of money is involved. I have managed to get where I am today, wherever that may be, by my talent and looks such as they both are. I do know of girls who have worked their way up on their backs, and although most of them have fallen by the wayside there are a few that have survived. But at least I know that I did it on my own.

In 1980 I did a TV series called *Triangle*. This was quite an experience – though for a change I am not speaking of the casting couch variety! It was the first attempt at filming TV drama in a sort of Outside Broadcast manner. I was playing the purser on a ferry line; we used a real ferry with real passengers and a real crew, plus us, the pretend crew, pretend passengers and the camera unit. It was something of an ordeal trying to stay upright in a Force 12 gale as well as cope with passengers who were speaking Swedish and Dutch, public announcements coming over the tannoy system, and a cast and crew that were working in shifts so they could take it in turns to throw up!

We used to spend eleven days on board plying the North Sea in October, November and December, possibly the worst months of the year. One looked out of one's porthole on to endless grey sky and grey sea, and had no idea of the location, time or even day of the week. Many members of the cast and the technical crew were not good sailors, and for them it was ghastly. I discovered that I *was* a good sailor, but whether that was because I was the leading lady – and so of course the show had to go on – I cannot say.

Real passengers would approach me, dressed as I was in my purser's uniform, and ask me where we were and what time we were likely to dock at, say, Amsterdam. Worn out by the incredibly hectic schedule and the general misery of it all, I would turn to them and say in a world-weary manner, 'I haven't the faintest idea.' This cannot have done anything to inspire their confidence in the running of the ship! It was always a great joy when we reached Amsterdam after two weeks at sea and were allowed to amble freely through that beautiful city.

Very often on the boat I would go down into the hold early in the morning where the make-up department was installed and find the dock littered with prone bodies. One's first impression, at that time of day, was that they had all had rather too good a time in the bar the previous evening – something the make-up department are quite good at, especially when there are a lot of amenable actors around. But in this case, the prostrate figures were suffering greatly. I remember having to do my own make-up and addressing my remarks to the floor to find out what the continuity was for the first scene of the day, since my make-up girl was enduring the tortures of the damned and quite unable to assist.

Despite some of the apparently negative things I have said about that side of the profession, my work in TV and films has involved much more than randy casting directors and seasick film crews. The great plus for me is that it has given me a very high media profile which I use as necessary when I am engaged in that part of my career that I really care about – the theatre, and in particular the British Actors' Theatre Company.

The idea of the company was thrust on me quite unex-

21

pectedly. The whole thing started off one blazing hot day in California. I was sitting in the house I was renting with my friend Jenny Agutter, gazing out at the brown scorched landscape that was the lower regions of Griffith Park. It was situated somewhere below the Hollywood sign and painted a rather interesting shade of yellow ochre. I had come to the end of my current storyline in *Dynasty* and had been informed by the studio that my services would not be required again until the end of the series, when I would possibly be in four episodes. This meant kicking my heels in Hollywood for a couple of months. I had been offered a couple of television roles, neither of them particularly exciting, and a new play at the Mark Taper Theatre. The latter held some interest for me, although I wasn't that enamoured of the part.

Suddenly the small green plastic frog by my side burped several times. In other words the phone was ringing. I picked up the offending animal and held its gaping mouth to my ear – I always felt slightly ridiculous addressing my remarks down the throat of this idiotic instrument. The voice on the other end was my agent ringing from London to tell me that I had been offered the parts of either Goneril or Regan in *King Lear* with Sir Antony Quayle's company, Compass. Was I interested? And if so which of the two parts would I prefer to play?

I had always had rather a hankering to play Goneril, the elder of the two sisters; being an elder sister myself I felt some sort of affinity with her. I also thought that she was possibly the more interesting character for me to play, since I would normally be more natural casting for Regan. Goneril is married to a good man and I feel has become corrupted over the years, whereas Regan seems to me more of a psychopath married to an equally bad, mad husband. For although it is Goneril who suggests that Gloucester's eyes are put out, it is Regan who is actually there when the ghastly deed is done.

I accepted the job with alacrity and requested a meeting with the studio bosses to inform them of my decision. They seemed puzzled, not to say perplexed, that I could possibly prefer to go home to go on tour with a classical drama instead of remaining in Hollywood to earn the big bucks. This aspect of the whole thing has mystified countless people whom I have spoken to, journalists and public alike. For me there was simply no choice. I have always had a philosophical attitude towards money: I have this fundamental belief that I will always manage to find the money from somewhere, but that my soul needs constant attention.

Exactly six weeks later, a little troop of strolling players could be descried toiling up the side of a mountain, albeit a small one, in the Derbyshire Peak District. The air was biting shrewdly – in fact it was freezing, and underfoot there was a great deal of slithery mud and the occasional snowdrift. I had already fallen flat on my back twice in the murky slime, had been almost up to my waist in icy water, and had left my ears a couple of miles further back on what looked like an ancient trackway. I was the only woman on this little expedition, which consisted of nine members of the *King Lear* company headed by Peter Woodward, who was playing Edgar in the production. We had opened the previous week and were determined to enjoy our Sunday off. Woodward's idea of enjoyment was to drag this disparate little group of thespians on a ten-mile route march across wild, unwelcoming terrain. He, however, was not amongst those present, but if one shaded one's eyes and gazed ahead he could be discerned as a speck on the horizon, occasionally turning to burst into a frenetic display of semaphore urging us onwards. About half way through this ordeal, after we had all passed through the pain barrier, Woodward very obligingly sat atop a little knoll to wait for us to catch up with him. Thankfully we collapsed and partook of various bits of survival food, nuts and chocolates and the like.

After this brief respite, he fell in beside me as we tramped along, arms swinging and getting into the rhythm of the whole thing. Suddenly he said, 'I'm thinking of starting a theatre company. Are you interested?'

Now, I am not a woman to be easily disarmed. I pride myself on being able to rise to any occasion, however preposterous.

'Yes,' I retorted immediately. 'I'll ring my solicitor tomorrow and put my house on the market.'

Peter threw back his head and laughed immoderately.

'I'm serious,' I said. 'I'll do it.' And I did.

Six months and a great deal of trauma later, we opened in *The Taming of the Shrew* at the Alexandra Theatre, Birmingham. I think it was probably the most exciting night of my life. The next day we got the sort of notices that one dreams about, and the British Actors' Theatre Company was born.

Given my background – five generations in the theatre – it had long been a cherished ambition of mine to start a theatre company. But without the American experience behind me – I had just spent my first few months in Hollywood filming *Dynasty* – I doubt if I would ever have achieved it. But Americans seem to be full of self-confidence, bursting with it in fact, and this is something I learnt from them: that anything, but anything, is possible if you believe in it. Self-belief and self-esteem are two of the most important assets if one is to survive, let alone succeed, in this bizarre world. Setting up a theatre company requires a monumental amount of determination, hard work and that essential total self-belief. Like any other business venture, it is necessary to research the market, find the product and then persuade people that they want it. Providing that one aims for excellence and the workmanship is of a high quality, one is in with a chance of success.

They were heady days, those early times during our very first production. We were breaking all the theatrical rules. For a start, we had no money. We had borrowed a lump sum from the bank to set up the production and were relying on the small guarantees we had from each theatre to pay the actors' wages. I was permanently armed with a needle and thread and a thimble and could be found at any time of day or night frantically sewing yet another Elizabethan costume. With amazing forwighting, Peter had purchased a set from *The Prisoner of Zenda* which he had been appearing in at Chichester two years previously. This was revamped and repainted to accommodate our view of Padua and Verona in the late sixteenth century. The costumes were bright and colourful and so were the performances.

The one thing that audiences all over the country, and indeed abroad, have commented on is the high energy level of our productions. This was established in our first *Shrew*. I had worked on three productions of the play previously and so was very familiar with the text and had very strong ideas about how we should stage it. We did not use a director for our first venture and the combined artistic input of the company was extraordinary. Wonderfully imaginative and anarchic ideas flowed constantly and we all found it a most exhilarating way in which to work. It was difficult and contentious, of course, but ultimately rewarding, because what the audience saw when the curtain went up was the actors' collective realization of Shakespeare's play. Even when we do use a director with our productions, we are now so used to expressing our own ideas that the actors' input has become a major integral part of our work.

These ideas go right across the board, and if I feel I am right about something I want to add into a production I will fight tooth and nail to get it done. One of these obsessions gave rise to a condition known as 'The Pink Hat Syndrome', coined by a brilliant comic performer, Nicholas Day, after an incident in Brighton. He was giving a superb performance as Tranio in that first BATCO production of *The Shrew*, but I like to think that I have contributed in a small way to his considerable expertise.

For most of the play the character has to dress up as his master, and we had the idea that he should borrow his master's

25

very, very best suit of clothes. Thus it was that Nick was an Elizabethan vision in cream leather and strawberry pink suede. He was wearing make-up and earrings and looked superb. However, for my money I felt the whole ensemble should have been topped with a wonderful Elizabethan hat. Nick disagreed: he felt he looked fine the way he was and didn't need to worry about the hat. He had, however, said that although he was enjoying the part he felt that something was missing. I knew precisely what it was. It was that pink hat. And I was determined that just such a hat would be found.

After the matinee performance at the Theatre Royal I whisked out into Hannington's, the local department store, and to my great joy found a length of strawberry pink silk that exactly matched the hue in his costume. I then rushed to an antique market and found some glorious, dusty pink feathers, including a piece of drooping osprey. Quickly I rustled up one of those Elizabethan pancake-style hats out of the pink silk and sewed on the feathers so that they stuck out at right-angles in a manner potentially lethal to any passing fellow actor. The drooping osprey I positioned so that it fell slightly over the left eye. I pinned the bright jewelled brooch where the feathers were stitched and presented Nick with this confection. He was amazed and delighted and wore it that night, and brought the house down. He was profuse in his gratitude and credited me with having supplied the missing element from his otherwise glorious performance. Thus it is that the phrase 'The Pink Hat Syndrome' has passed down into theatrical phraseology, hopefully to be emulated by future generations of actors.

I am very particular about the way my actors look on stage. If they are going to be brightly lit, I think it is essential that they look superb, otherwise there is no point to any of it. The audience come to see as well as hear a wonderful show, and they must not be disappointed.

When we were doing Vanbrugh's *The Relapse*, we had some

glorious costumes. My leading man, Richard Heffer, looked superb in almond green silk; ruffles at the neck and wrists, long blond curling hair tied at the nape of the neck and superb thigh-high leather boots. Richard is a splendid figure of a man and he looked a dreamboat. Unfortunately he was persuaded by one of his fellow actors that the boots did not look right and that the proper way to wear them was turned down at the knee.

So, I made an entrance to find the man with whom I was supposed to be madly in love wandering around the stage in what appeared to be a pair of milk pails. It threw me quite badly. I almost dried and certainly fluffed. I became completely riveted by this ghastly apparition and played the scene with inwardly mounting fury at the sight of this travesty. At the end of the scene I stormed into his dressing room and let rip. To my enormous surprise, he let rip back at me. I am not used to this and it almost took the wind out of my sails, but having found a good sparring partner I went for it. We both screamed, yelled, shrieked and shouted at each other for about ten minutes. Indeed, it was said that the row could be heard on stage even though we were a couple of flights up in a remote dressing room.

Most dressing rooms are remote in many of the big theatres, since theatres are almost always designed without any thought for the actors' need to get to and from the stage for quick changes. Conditions backstage are on the whole fearful, even in very modern theatres, where in many instances they seem to have forgotten that there are actors. In one famous case a brand-new theatre was designed and completed without any dressing rooms for the actors at all. What they thought all those people in the very comfortable auditorium were coming to see, God alone knows. But I digress. . . .

Trembling with fury, Richard and I then had to go on stage and play a passionate love scene. It is conceivable that this particular encounter had rather more emotional content than usual. It is to his lasting credit that he reappeared on stage with the boots properly pulled up, and that he has not only forgiven me for my ridiculous outburst (which I have to say in my own defence was simply because I wanted him to look good) but that he has shown signs of extreme friendliness towards me, and we even did a nude bed scene together in *Howard's Way* when he was cast opposite me again!

If I had a choice, I would spend the whole of my life appearing in nothing but Shakespeare and possibly some of the early classical writers such as Sheridan, Middleton and Farquhar. Shakespeare is the love of my life; I think he is simply the greatest genius that has ever lived and I want everyone to share this joyous experience, and so by appearing from time to time in the more popular television series I have built up a potential theatre audience. Many of those who come to see me in the theatre come up to me in the bar or at the stage door afterwards and express their delight at what they have seen. Many say that not only have they never seen Shakespeare before, but they have never even been to a theatre before. So I feel that my double life as classical actress/glamour girl has its rewards.

2

Dynasty Diary

My ultimate glamour role is Caress in *Dynasty*, and there is absolutely no doubt that it changed my life. The world of Hollywood and in particular that of Hollywood soaps was so new to me, so extraordinary, that I kept a kind of diary of my feelings and responses to each new situation. I have called on those diary notes to fill in the details of my recollections.

There were many times when I was younger when I might have gone to Hollywood. My agent's office was frequently being assaulted by the arrival of highly dramatic telegrams which read something like 'SEND PHOTOS O'MARA RE BURTON PICTURE URGENT.' His staff would be thrown into total confusion and panic for several days, then everything would settle down again and we would never hear another word. So to go for the first time at the age of forty-six was, I think, remarkable in itself. Of course I didn't *look* forty-six, any more than I look my age now.

Even so, theree's also no doubt that I was called out there largely due to the success of Joan Collins, who is the great trailblazer for the 'older woman'.

In the period just before I went to Hollywood my life was a disaster area in every way. My career was at an all-time low, my personal life – that is, my relationship at that time – was not working out, and I was becoming aware that I was physically no longer quite so young as I was – a fact I found very depressing. To be suddenly summoned to Tinsel Town was really quite invigorating and stimulating and started me off on a roller-coaster ride which is still thundering along some fairly awe-inspiring rails.

Sunday, 20 October
My arrival at LA Airport was unpromising. I was regarded with deep suspicion by the immigration officer– suspicion bordering on intense personal hatred – and for one glorious moment I thought I was going to be denied entry into the country. He found it necessary to enlist the aid of his superior officer, who muttered that his fears were unfounded. As I stood there nervously awaiting my fate I wanted to tell them that, far from being an indesirable alien, I could show them stacks of porno-graphic fan mail proving beyond doubt my eminent desirability. He asked me the nature of my work.

'I'm an actress,' I said, curbing the impulse to add, 'But it's open to debate.'

The look he gave me was chilling.

I also resisted the urge to jolly things along by saying, 'Is that a gun in your pocket or are you just pleased to see me?' as I realised that it was indeed a gun in his pocket and this boy was clearly not into older women.

After what seemed an eternity, he snapped shut my passport and with a look of deep contempt gestured to me to get out of his hair. I joined my agent, Michael Ladkin, who was looking apprehensive at the baggage collection point. As indeed he might – the vision of mega-dollars having temporarily gone out of focus before his very eyes.

Things got better after that. I signed my first autograph for a charming black porter who thought I was the bee's knees. I mentally apologised to President Reagan's portrait, as I passed it, for my extreme impudence in presuming to invade his territory (the immigration officer, I was now convinced, was trained to look into people's souls and *knew* that I was an unwilling visitor).

We waited on the pavement for our car to pick us up and I just had time to observe sights and smells which reminded me of Tangier, when a white house on wheels drew alongside and we scrambled aboard. We did not avail ourselves of the numerous amenities on offer (television, cocktail cabinet, telephone, gymnasium etc.), but stared bleakly out of the smoked glass windows at the gargantuan hoardings lining the freeway.

The Beverly Hills Hotel turned out to be an old-fashioned establishment done out in very dark green, which I found forest-like and reassuring. One expensive hotel is very much like another on the inside, so once in my room I drew the curtains, shut out the palm trees and turned on the TV set. To my utter delight, after trying about fifteen channels of junk, I found a programme about music and had about forty-five minutes of Scarlatti, Viotti, Clementi and various other baroque babies. This, plus the fact that it poured with rain all Monday, softened the culture shock somewhat. Michael made several phone calls, then we met for a drink in the Polo Lounge. This is just a polite name for the local pick-up joint. We stared for a while at the numerous whores and their prospective clients, exchanged a few desultory remarks and decided to call it a day at nine o'clock.

Monday, 21 October

I slept fitfully for almost twelve hours, then tried to ease the tension in my back by soaking in a hot bath. I went down to breakfast where I found Michael already seated. The dining room was adjacent to the Polo Lounge but was really a sort of loggia that looked out on to a patio overhung with the gnarled and twisted branches of a tree which stood in the centre of the patio. The whole effect was one of pleasant shade and foliage.

Thus refreshed (I only had tea), we took a taxi to the less expensive part of town to get me some heated rollers as they had confiscated my butane gas-powered curling tongs at Gatwick. I also needed an alarm clock since I had no way of knowing the time, particularly as my internal clock had gone haywire. The sleazy tawdriness of the area appalled me: everything was brash and tacky. I managed to get the articles I wanted and beat a hasty retreat to the hotel.

There were messages waiting for us from my American agent, informing us that after an initial meeting with him over lunch my presence was required at the studio to meet the writers and one of the producers. I would also be needed in wardrobe. Michael told me to put on a dress, as this was considered *de rigueur*. I obliged and, feeling wildly over-dressed, took a cab with him to the American agent's offices, where we were welcomed enthusiastically. With Harry, who runs the New York office (your softly spoken, cultured American, silver-haired, suntanned, impeccably dressed) was his right-hand man in charge of the LA office. He buzzed in and out of the office answering vital calls and sending telexes, then finally rushed off to a meeting that could no longer be denied his presence. After meeting the rest of the office staff we went to lunch, where we sat in a booth on a leather banquette and Harry and I exchanged pleasantries. I've been a vegetarian for years, and don't like to eat too much anyway. They could manage a vegetarian sandwich, but brought me one big enough for ten people! I consumed less than one-tenth and then we set off for the studio.

There I was taken up to the office of Diane Lean, who actually *runs* the show. She turned out to be a thin, tense, attractive woman in her fifties. She was absolutely charming to me but I would hate to incur her displeasure, let alone her wrath. She took me to meet the writers, a husband-and-wife team who think up the storylines. They proved to be darlings: he a thin, gawky, soft-spoken, retiring man with pale brown, almost beige, wavy hair, and she a Junoesque bouncy brunette who was vociferous in her welcome. She admitted to identifying closely with Alexis, and they both admitted that they made it up as they went along.

After being given a cup of coffee (of which I was allowed two sips) and a brief discussion of my storyline (I mentioned that I thought Cassandra a wonderful name – it fell on stony ground and I'm stuck with Caress) I was dismissed to wardrobe, where a darling girl, Sunny by name, greeted me with a dazzling smile and a rail full of some of the most hideous frocks I have ever seen. I tried on the least offensive, a creation in lime green satin and magenta taffeta topped with a brown organza meringue. The door opened and the designer, Dylan Cooper, appeared.

'Stunning!' he said. 'Just terrific!' and approached me, deft fingers twitching. He shoved the material this way and that, pinned it in here and pulled it out there and, having made it his own, declared it fit for the cameras.

Diane was summoned. She strode in through the door and shrieked: 'She *can't* wear that! It's too, too . . . .' Words failed her.

A person of uncertain gender then oozed into the fitting room, covered in gold trinkets and baubles and having apparently absent-mindedly placed his sitting room rug on his head. He (for it was Harold the hairdresser) took one look at me and uttered the ominous words: 'Joan wore that on a Sony commercial last week.'

'I *knew* it,' squawked Diane.

'Are you *sure*?' ventured Dylan, keen to get back to more important matters.

'*Positive*, said Harold, relishing his role as Nemesis, 'I *know* because *I* did her hair!' And, having ruined everyone's afternoon, he oozed out again.

The offending garment was ripped from my back and I was then shoved in and out of various other monstrosities. With each new frock I was scrutinised and commented upon as though I was not present. I began to feel like Alice in Wonderland, with Diane as the Queen of Hearts yelling: 'Off with that dress!' Whenever there was a lull in the proceedings Dylan as the Mad Hatter desperately tried to placate her. Poor Sunny was definitely the March Hare, going demented trying to make *something* work, and I noticed that Michael had gratefully assumed the role of the Dormouse and was quietly nodding off in the corner. It was finally decided that there was nothing suitable, and Sunny and I would have to go shopping the following day.

At this point Bill, the make-up man, arrived. Charming, unassuming, softly spoken, humorous and slightly portly, he was like a dozen other make-up men I've worked with, a reassuring familiar figure. He drew me to the fitting-room mirror under the lights. Looking like Nancy Reagan after a bad night, I told him to brace himself and do what he could. He said not to worry, he would make me look gorgeous.

Michael and I were glad at last to be able to get back to the hotel as jet-lag had hit us. So we flung ourselves into our studio car (a relatively modest chariot) and were whisked off to the hotel where we soon called it another day. It was, to my delight, pouring with rain.

Tuesday, 22 October
After breakfast Sunny arrived and we all three set off shopping. We spent all morning in every expensive boutique and depart-

ment store in LA, ending up in Giorgio's – a very exclusive shop where they were playing thirties' music and a marble and copper bar was dispensing free coffee topped with cream and cinnamon, and ice-cold beer. We partook of their bounty and I tried on a ravishing black velvet number with black grosgrain ruffles around the shoulders, set off by diamond and sapphire necklace and earrings. Armed with that and other tasteful garments culled from our morning's travail Sunny returned to the studio and we went back for a late lunch.

A character by the name of Cherub Jackson briefly came into my life today. Michael had met her last time he was in LA and is by way of being her London agent. She is about thirty-five, blonde and reminiscent of an early Dyan Cannon. Cherub skipped up the entrance path and steps to the hotel and bounded light as thistledown into the lobby (a girl clearly used to appearing in television commercials for vitamin pills or shampoo or something healthy). She squealed with delight on seeing Michael and embraced him enthusiastically. He then introduced me, and she gazed at me with skin aglow and eyes shining.

'Oh, are you my friend?' she said excitedly. 'Yes, you are my friend, I know it,' she exclaimed without waiting for a reply.

Then she clasped me to her for what seemed an eternity. I disentangled myself after what I thought was a decently polite interval.

Michael said, 'This is Kate's first visit to LA. . . .'

'Be a happy guest,' breathed Cherub. 'Know yourself, fill your space and be a happy guest.'

'OK,' I said, keen to finish the conversation and put a lot of space between myself and this deranged peroxide number who plainly didn't have a marble she could call her own. But she didn't let up.

'In this world of ours', she continued, 'we have to know our time and what we are, and when our time comes we have to fill our space, we have to be at peace with ourselves and our space. Be happy, my friend, be a happy guest.'

I gazed wildly round the lobby for means of escape, and finally I turned to Michael, 'What the fuck is she talking about?' I said, trying to make it sound humorous. Rude, I know, but she was beginning to aggravate me. Michael laughed in an embarrassed way and I decided to leave them to it. 'I'm sorry, jet-lag,' I said, and beat a hasty retreat.

I spent the rest of the day going over my lines and catching up on sleep, as I had a 4.30 call the next morning. Even though I now had my alarm clock I was taking no chances, so I called the desk and asked for an early morning call.

'Pardon me?' said the operator politely.

I repeated that I would like an early morning call.

'You wanna make a call in the morning?' She seemed surprised. 'Oh, you wanna *wake-up* call, *fine*.'

'Thank you.'

'Surely.'

Wednesday, 23 October
I slept fitfully again, but was up by the time I got my 4.30 'wake-up call'. At 5.30 I was at the studios. They pulled my hair off my face and gave me very little make-up. I then had to get into my prison garb – a shapeless garment in grey with a long skirt and high neck, and some really naff flat Mexican plaited leather shoes – and was taken downstairs to the set. Here I was introduced to what seemed like thousands, of technicians, all very friendly, and the director, an ex-actress named Betty Maguire.

My gaoler was a Mexican called Juan who was keen to go over the lines with me. This was just as well, as he plainly did not know them and in any case I was nervous. We got on to the set and rehearsed; Betty seemed pleased, suggested a couple of things and then called for the stand-ins. She then decided she wanted to do a very complicated opening shot which would take ages to light, but she was determined and so there was a hiatus of about an hour. Finally we got the first shot done and the second with Juan blowing his lines every time. Fortunately I had my wits about me by this time and was busy learning the names of at least twenty of the crew.

We were setting up the third shot when a very pretty, very thin blonde suddenly appeared in front of me and clasped my hand. This proved to be Linda Evans. 'I've just come to say hello and welcome,' she smiled, 'and to see if you were all right.' She was wearing blue jeans, a pale blue shirt and white fringed moccasin-type boots, and had two rollers in her hair at the sides. She looked and was enchanting. A few set-ups later John Forsythe wandered on to the set – also, he claimed, to welcome me.

By this time, thanks to Betty wanting fancy shots and Juan blowing his lines, we were two hours behind schedule. Not a very auspicious beginning, I thought. However, we finally got the last shot done and then I went off to make-up to have myself made glamorous as we were having *more* costume fittings in the afternoon. Bill, the make-up man, made me look fine, and I decided to leave my own preferred make-up details until the next day when we were shooting my first 'entrance' as Caress. The hairdresser was called Lynne – a very nice girl who took me on as Harold decided that coping with Joan was about as much as he could handle.

When I was almost glamorised Linda Evans popped her head round the door to pass a few complimentary remarks, then she was gone. A few moments later the door burst open and Stephanie Beacham appeared. In about five minutes flat she managed to give me a rundown on her new lifestyle, code of behaviour at the studio and her two phone numbers (her place at Malibu as well as the one in town) before she too buzzed off.

I had been given the use of Diahann Carroll's dressing room, the walls of which boasted framed nominations for various awards, letters from two members of the Kennedy Clan thanking her for services rendered but not specified, and other such ego-trip memorabilia. I was in the throes of casting a jaundiced eye over all this when Bill put his head in and said, 'Would you like to meet your sister?'

'Rather!' I enthused.

I heard him go two doors along (Linda Evans had the dressing room next door) and repeat the question. There was a sort of squeal followed by a rat-tat-tat of determined high heels on hard, shiny surface, and the next moment Joanie was asking if she could come in and sit down. She was clad entirely in cream – trousers, shirt, scarf, shoes – and gold, and wearing not a scrap of make-up. She looked stunning. Her hair was scraped back off her face and secured with an elastic band.

Joan flung herself on to the black leather sofa and asked me how I was getting on. Did I know anything about the storyline? She was somewhat alarmed, she said, about her background being revealed. She'd been playing Alexis as having a rather good upbringing, and if now I was about to reveal otherwise – well, it was a bit throwing to say the least. Where was I staying? She looked surprised when I told her. Were 'they' paying?

'Good Lord, yes,' I said.

'Good,' she said.

I told her I thought she was wonderful in the show – and meant it – she seemed pleased.

She thought it would be a good idea if I had an affair with 'Dex' – that would stir things up a bit, she thought. Suddenly she could hear her phone ringing in her room. She let out another squeal and leaped up. 'I must go – I've a dozen messages to take. I can't wait for our first scene together – they're all longing for it – the Battle of the British Bitches,' she laughed. 'The BBB!' And she tore off down the corridor.

A little while later I bumped into her and Linda, both fully made up and dressed and both looking glorious, Linda in black and white and Joan in red.

After that I went off for another costume fitting. I was put into the gorgeous black number and Dylan Cooper was called. 'Well, it is just *sensational!*' he said.

Diane Lean was summoned. She stopped dead in the doorway and put a hand to her brow. 'What is this?'

Dylan turned away exasperated. 'Oh, my Gahd!' he said, 'for heaven's sake, if we have to worry about what every other woman in the entire cast is wearing . . . .'

'No, just what *Joan* wears, she mustn't have the Joan Look!' There followed a heated debate, after which the divine black dress was removed from my person, never to be seen again – except, I imagine, on Joan.

After this they fished out a little swathed gold lamé number with matching frilled shawl. Again Diane was called, again she had a turn and said Joan had worn something similar.

'Yes, but that was *four years ago,*' said the despairing Dylan. Another fierce argument ensued, which ended with Dylan almost swearing on oath that the one Joan had worn was *nothing* like this one. Diane accepted this reluctantly and we all went our ways.

When I got back to the hotel I went to my room where I watched *Yes Minister* and *The French Lieutenant's Woman* which I had not seen before, not being a cinema-goer. I then did a good session on my lines for the morrow and went to bed.

Thursday, 24 October

I was beginning to get over my jet-lag by now, so was able to wake up at the proper time and joined Michael for breakfast. I then washed my hair and set it as – incredible though it may seem – they don't have facilities for hair-washing at the studios. Warner's studios themselves look much like Elstree at first glance, only they are painted a hideous mud colour all over. And the dressing rooms are tiny – not like dear old ABPC or Pinewood, where one had an enormous sitting room with a bed and private bathroom or at least a shower and loo. Not a bit of it. Here there is only a public loo, which I find quite extraordinary.

However, today we were on location in South Pasadena and I had a late call. So off I went with my driver, who gave me a conducted tour and was most informative. We arrived at City Hall in Pasadena, which has Baroque pretention, and I sought out the make-up trailer. No one was ready for me, so I went to my own trailer and waited, going over my lines again. Finally my hairdresser arrived and said she would Carmen my hair. This she did, and very well too. She is a pretty, quiet, shy girl who knows her job. Soon after this they announced that Betty had got ahead of schedule and we were all moving to the next location. So the second assistant director – a really nice, jolly, bouncy girl called Kerry, who is full of beans and also very good at her job – Bill, Lynne and I all piled into a car and were driven there. The new location proved to be a most beautiful house set in lovely grounds at the top of a sweeping drive and surrounded with trees. It was built in 1902 in a sort of quasi-Queen Anne style but with the odd Art Nouveau touch here and there and occasionally a hint of Spanish influence. However, despite these mixed origins the overall effect was one of quiet, subdued splendour. There were superb antiques everywhere, lovely if obscure oil paintings, an old gold silk carpet, parquet flooring and chandeliers. A fountain was playing in the inner hall and there was a small staircase down which I was to make my first entrance.

After I was made up, I did my first rehearsal with my hair in curlers and in my make-up robe and slippers – both provided by the studio. I then walked back through the gardens to my trailer and changed into my gold lamé number with the frilly shawl and gold high heels. I was given a bronze necklace and earrings, my hair was tarted around and backcombed and lacquered, tweaked and teased within an inch of its life, and I was proclaimed ready for my grand entrance. I caused a minor sensation on the set – but technicians are the same the world over.

The actor with whom I was playing the scene was a tall, distinguished-looking man in his late fifties called Robert Rhill; he was very good, had obviously worked in the theatre, and played the scene really well. However, when it came to his close-ups he too started blowing his lines. I deduced from this that the problem is that actors simply don't get enough practice out here and therefore lose confidence when under pressure. When we weren't shooting the scene we retired into a cool conservatory (it was boiling outside) and went over our lines there. We finished the scene about 5.45 and I was driven back to the hotel, where ABC TV rang inviting me to the *Dynasty/Colbys* bash.

Friday, 28 October
More wardrobe fittings! I went to the studio and tried on a snazzy little red suit for my first scene with Joanie at La Mirage. It was nipped in at the waist to fit me snugly – the skirt was made less flared and pads were put in the shoulders to give me the current Hollywood look. Sunny had also managed to get the most wonderful grey wool trenchcoat that was several sizes too large. It was ruthlessly reduced to my size and looked divine. I prayed that it would meet with the approval of the Red Queen and the Mad Hatter. A runner was despatched, and several minutes elapsed as apparently they were looking at the daily rushes.

Suddenly Diane was at the door. She came rushing in and kissed me on both cheeks, exclaiming that my scene in the gold lamé dress was a triumph. It transpired that screams of delight had gone up in the viewing room on my first appearance. After this (in my opinion) excessive display of emotion, she dis-

41

covered that she *loved* the red suit and thought the trenchcoat *adorable*. Dylan appeared, and agreed wholeheartedly. Dear Sunny was flushed with triumph.

I spent the rest of the day getting ready for the *Dynasty/Colbys* 'do'. At seven o'clock Michael and I were downing our pre-bash drinks to allay our nerves, then went out to our waiting limousine. We arrived at the Beverly Wilshire and climbed out into a sea of people, popping flashbulbs and throngs of reporters. I knew they were not interested in me and was just slipping in, I thought unnoticed, when suddenly a lone photographer yelled my name. There was nothing for it – I had to turn and pose before following Michael into the hotel.

We entered a room full of glittering people – not one of whom did we know. We grabbed a drink and then found ourselves accosted by a number of people who were all ecstatic about my rushes – as the producers were among those who were eulogizing we allowed ourselves to feel optimistic for the first time.

After this we all drifted into dinner. More or less everyone else was there, though, including Ricardo Montalban who I had been given to understand was playing my boyfriend. Among the 'Colbys' I spotted David Hedison, whom I had worked with in 1970. We had done a TV play for Anglia directed by Alvin Rakoff, in which I had played Richard Johnson's wife and David had played my American lover. He didn't seem too pleased to see me amongst the present throng.

I found my table in the dining room and we all sat down. After the starter, one of the producers got up and made a speech and introduced the other producer to the assembly. He chuntered on for a while about this and that, and then the ABC representative got up and the whole thing turned into a mutual admiration society song of praise. After this the first producer decided to introduce each member of both casts to the multitude. I prayed that I wouldn't be included in this mass exposure, but to my horror I heard an introduction that began with, 'The newest member of the *Dynasty* cast, an English actress . . .' and saw the spotlight swinging over in my direction. Michael pushed me to my feet, so I bowed and smiled hopefully to the room and caught a glimpse over in my direction and politely joining in the general applause. The whole ghastly scene easily surpassed my worst nightmares.

The rest of the evening passed off without incident and I had time to notice that Katherine Ross (a Colbyite) had cut off most of her beautiful auburn hair to shoulder length and had it permed, and that Linda Evans was wearing a red evening suit with a black leaf-like design in sequins over one shoulder. I chatted up the writers who were sitting next to me at our table, and was very thankful when Michael suggested that, as various other people were leaving, we might as well go too. The food was fairly inedible – as is always the case at these functions – and in any case we were sick to death of the *Dynasty* theme, which the band had played almost continuously for most of the evening.

As we were leaving, Dylan came up to me with Barbara Stanwyck on his arm and congratulated me on my rushes. Then he said, 'Barbara, I'd like you to meet Kate O'Mara. Kate, this is Barbara.'

Miss Stanwyck took my hand and said, 'Barbara?'

Nolan said, 'No, *you're* Barbara. This is Kate, she's playing Joan's sister.'

'Who's Joan?' enquired Miss Stanwyck, nonplussed.

'She plays Alexis.'

'Alexis?' wondered Miss Stanwyck, totally baffled.

'Oh, never mind,' said Dylan wearily.

'I don't know who *anyone* is,' complained Miss Stanwyck with desperation. Dylan led her away, a beaten man who was exhibiting all the signs of having spent a lifetime of coping with difficult women.

We came across Diahann Carroll on our way but she totally

ignored me, so we made our way to the front of the hotel where we found a dispirited little group of extremely famous people all waiting anxiously for their limousines to come and whisk them off into the night. Our turn came sooner than the rest and we sank back into the plush upholstery with a sigh of relief.

Saturday, 26 October
Michael had hired a car and was determined that I was going to see the Californian coastline, so armed with a map and with me as navigator we set off for Malibu. This was a vast disappointment and reminded me of Shoreham-on-Sea in the sixties after a particularly hectic visit from the Mods and Rockers. On the way we made a mental note of the whereabouts of Stewart Granger's abode (he invited us for supper) and then drove on to Venice, which was even worse than Malibu. Michael appeared enchanted by the place, but I don't know when I have encountered anywhere more dirty, tawdry, sleazy, full of junkies, con-men, reprobates, mindless alcoholics, tramps and charlatans. The rejects of society – the debris, the misfits of the world.

Michael said, 'Isn't it fascinating? I wouldn't mind living here.'

I replied, 'Listen, you can see this any day of the week at throwing out time at the Dog and Fox in Wimbledon or in a Terry Hands production at the RSC for that matter, and save yourself the air fare.'

Michael was unconvinced, and we spent most of the day wandering up and down amongst this motley crew. He insisted that we have a drink on Malibu Beach in a fairly ghastly sort of café. The best part was gazing out of the picture windows, watching the gulls and sandpipers and suddenly seeing a school of dolphins disporting themselves in the waves, which reminded me of Cleopatra's lines in her eulogy about Antony after his death:

> . . . his delights
> Were dolphin-like; they show'd his back above
> The element they liv'd in. . . .

This made me homesick again and I gazed out to sea, trying not to think of dear Will Shakespeare and our mutual love of the English countryside and trying not to cry.

Finally it was time to go to Jimmy Granger's, who made us very welcome. He had cooked enough food for ten people and we did our best, but it was quite an effort! He gave us cheese on toast as an appetiser. Then cold asparagus with an amazing vinaigrette sauce. Plus avocados. Followed by spaghetti bolognaise with a special alternative sauce for me, a sort of ratatouille. Then chocolate mousse and strawberries and cream. I managed to eat a little of everything but not without a great deal of difficulty. He is not a man to be thwarted.

Stewart, still handsome, witty, amusing, fascinating, with a confidence bordering on arrogance, made a charming informal host. The corridors of his apartment were crammed with photographic evidence of his once staggering good looks and superb tall physique. There were shots of him in *Beau Brummel*, *The Prisoner of Zenda*, *King Solomon's Mines* and a dozen others. He was a good actor, too, but never recognised as such. I remember him in those films and thinking him the most handsome man I had ever seen with the exception, perhaps, of Errol Flynn. And I remember crying at the end of *Beau Brummel* and *Young Bess*, and the sadness remaining with me for ages afterwards. 'I wasn't a bad-looking chap, was I?' he said heartily as he showed us around his flat. I suddenly realised that I had seen every one of his films – and told him so, which pleased him. I even managed to quote a line he had to Peter Ustinov in *Beau Brummel*, and this plainly delighted him.

Immediately outside his bedroom door was a life-size photograph of himself in bathing trunks taken on a yacht, bronzed and young and beautiful (and knowing it!). 'Ah, yes,' he said, laughing. 'I show this to my girlfriends and say, "Now take a good look at this chap. Then close your eyes and imagine he's the fellow you're in bed with".'

Wednesday, 30 October
Today Michael has to leave Hollywood and go back to England. *All* my agents turned up at the hotel for a party for casting directors – they were giving themselves awards for casting! (I mean – PLEASE!) I happened to be in the lobby just as the lunch was finishing and bumped into my new agents, who instantly grabbed the opportunity and managed to introduce me to every important casting director in the business in the space of half an hour (they were waiting for their limos to collect them and in high good humour, being slightly pissed). The casting directors were all very charming and politely interested in me until my agents let it slip that I was a new regular in *Dynasty*, whereupon they all became *riveted* by me and paid me a great deal of attention.

Thursday, 31 October
As I was responsible for my own transport to the studio today, I had a cab standing by and arrived in beautiful time to do my first scene with Joanie and Gordon Thompson. I even had a chair with my name on it on set – something that has not happened to me for several years. Bill did a good job on my face; he's gradually catching on and taking my advice as to what needs doing to make me look presentable – I hope to have got my make-up the way I like it by my third episode.

Joanie was very sweet to me. She had invited me to a party at her place, which, as I was going home at the beginning of the week, I should have to miss. We had no exchange of dialogue in this, our first scene. It really consisted of me watching her covertly over breakfast at La Mirage – she unaware – and being spotted by Adam doing so.

46

DYNASTY DIARY

When we broke for lunch she and I had photos taken together for the *News of the World* this coming Sunday, 3 November. She chatted to me in a most friendly manner all the while. So far, so good. Diane also came on to the set and congratulated me on having my options picked up. I was never in any doubt about this eventuality, but then if I had known there were sixty girls up for this part I might not have been so sanguine about that either. Eight were eventually tested on videotape. Stephanie Beacham actually had to do a test in Hollywood as well. At least I was spared that.

There is no canteen or restaurant at Warner Bros and most people send out for food, but I had been overlooked. So I changed out of my red suit and black hat, put on my jumpsuit and wandered out into the blazing sunshine to find the catering truck which was behind the *Love Boat* stages. They had been making *Matt Houston* there until a few months ago, but the series is not finished so I've missed him (Lee Horsley that is). (Who he? Ed.)

I finally found the truck and asked politely for a banana sandwich with brown bread, if they had it.

The catering manager stared at me and said, 'How's that, sister?!'

I repeated my request and he said, 'Aw, got ya, you wanna banana on wheat – comin' up! Whaddya wan on it?'

'Just banana, thank you,' I replied timorously.

He shook his head disbelieving, but made it just the same!

Friday, 1 November
A special delivery arrived on Friday afternoon from the studio. They had written me in another scene at La Mirage, also to be shot on Monday. I was very pleased, because it shows they seem to have some confidence in me.

I spent the afternoon getting my flight organised and learning my new scene. Then in the evening I did a lot of sewing and watched a Lee Horsley movie – (Who he? Ed!)

Saturday, 2 November

Did absolutely bugger all. Sat out on the balcony most of the day writing. Spent the evening watching TV. American sit-com series are far, far better written than ours – they are wittier, sharper, funnier and do not rely on contrived situations for their plots. I saw in quick succession about five which are obviously long-running favourites, and they were all excellent. As a great treat I ordered hot chocolate in bed and listened to Benjamin Britten and did the *Observer* crossword. I read it from cover to cover, except the business section – I shall wait until I get my corporation going before I tackle that! Any money I make is going into my production company and will probably go the way of all flesh. As I intend to revive obscure Restoration and Jacobean plays in the theatre and do historical travelogues and a dramatised series on the dear old Anglo-Saxons on TV, this is probably a very accurate forecast.

Little did I realise as I sat there in bed in Hollywood that soon I would be doing exactly what I dreamed about in the theatre.

3

Who Is the Real Kate O'Mara?

My public image – which, as I've already said, I loathe – is very different from the real me. But people in the public eye are just like everyone else in that they have their likes and dislikes, their good side and their faults. This chapter is about me as I see myself – the real me underneath the public façade.

I lead a very pressurised, hectic life. This is partly out of necessity and partly out of choice – both physical and mental, and I am a workaholic. Work, of course, does stop one thinking too deeply about what the hell it's all about anyway – life, I mean. Whenever I go to the country these are thoughts that crowd in on me unbidden. The peace and space of the countryside make me wonder why I am tearing around and going nowhere. I have found no answer to this particular

49

conundrum – I don't think there is one. So I just continue on in my mad rush to the grave.

However, I do have moments of relaxation; these are very dear and precious to me, and I hug them close to me and enjoy them hugely. I have always been an early riser – I wake early and seldom lie a-bed. I bound up and immediately go to make a cup of tea and then I sit in my favourite place of the moment, either curled up on a sofa or warming my bum against an Aga, sipping a delicious brew of Lapsang Souchong with my one weakness, brown sugar, tons of it stirred liberally in. I have countless cups of tea in the morning in this manner, just watching the dawn, listening to the birds and thinking of nothing in particular and everything in general. It is my moment of quiet and contemplation and sets me up for the whole day. I like the idea that I am stealing a march on time and that I have these few precious moments before I need to start the business of the day.

Radio 3 usually starts at seven o'clock, so from that time onwards I have a musical accompaniment to my cogitation. I am passionate about music and always have been. My first ambition, theatrical background notwithstanding, was to become a concert pianist. At about the age of thirteen I certainly had the ability, but sadly not the talent. I suspect I would have had the application, because I have found that I have the facility to apply myself wholeheartedly to whatever project I undertake.

I cannot imagine life without music. It soothes me, inspires me, exhilarates me and orders my life. I remember being present at the Conservatoire in Nice when there were student examinations in progress. These took place at the gorgeous little theatre. I sat all day in that darkened, glinting place listening to countless renditions of Beethoven's 4th Piano Concerto. I was completely entranced and did not want to leave.

If I am in a state of emotional turbulence, which I usually am, I find Bach (that is Johann Sebastian) or any of the Baroque composers very therapeutic. I think this is because their music is so ordered. There is nearly always a theme, and then variations on that theme, and finally the whole thing is brought to a satisfactory conclusion. It is almost mathematical in its precision and I find that reasuring when I am troubled. This kind of music provides me with the sort of emotional security that I crave, and seldom find.

If, however, I am feeling reasonably content but tired from the day's exertions, it is very pleasant to indulge in some Mozart by way of entertainment. Two of Bach's sons, Johann Christian and Carl Phillip Emanual, are also very diverting. When I need joyous, relaxing music I find that many of the eighteenth-century composers fulfil this need. If I am out of work or there is a lull in proceedings, a hiatus of one sort or another, I seek inspiration from more recent composers. I am devoted to Vaughan Williams, Richard Strauss and Michael Tippett amongst others. In lighter vein I turn to Percy Grainger and Delius, and when I need something dramatic, Beethoven, Brahms and Rachmaninov. If I am really bored I can cope with avant-garde music: I can tackle Berio, Stockhausen, Henze and Birtwistle and even Alban Berg.

As for pop music, I can take it – but in small doses. I like good old slurpy romantic stuff and smoochy ballads, and every now and again something in the charts appeals to me or takes me back to my youth when I was young and easy.

I adore bopping, letting my hair down and doing a great deal of free-wheeling. I never go to night clubs and seldom go out to supper. There are, of course, exceptions to this. When I am on tour with a play or in a West End theatre there is a desperate need to unwind after the show, particularly if it is a very demanding piece. I am inclined to go bopping only in the provinces, for the simple reason that if one goes in the West End one attracts a lot of attention from the paparazzi, who are ever-vigilant in their quest for tabloid fodder. A lady of uncertain age accompanied by a much younger man and performing something akin to St Vitus dance in the manner of a wild dervish is high on their list of priorities.

I have absolutely no inhibitions and enjoy myself enormously. I can outdance and outlast girls twenty years my junior, and have done so on many occasions. I remember a party I gave during the tour of *King Lear* when we were in Blackpool. The late, beloved Antony Quayle came in with his dear little dog Tiger and watched in amazement while I performed these strange rites. At five o'clock the following morning the various younger members of the company were all supine on the floor and semi-comatose, whilst I was still going strong. I have enormous staying power and get myself on a high without the aid of alcohol or any other stimulants.

On the whole I do not go to first nights or premieres, because I hate to attract attention. And I always feel so sorry for the actors, who are under such enormous pressure at a first performance. I would much rather see them later in the run when they have played it in and are more relaxed.

I had a most memorable and unusual view of one particular first night in the West End. It was when appearing in *The Italian Girl* at Wyndham's Theatre – the occasion of that awful practical joke on Paul Scofield – and John Osborne's new play *Hotel in Amsterdam* was opening at the adjoining New Theatre (now the Albery). In the middle of our performance my co-star Timothy West led me across the overhead linking passageway between the two theatres until we were above the stage of the New, where the first night performance was in progress. I can recall now, vividly, the unbelievable tension and energy that came winging its way up to us where we stood, hardly daring to breath, as Paul Scofield, Judy Parfitt, Isabel Dean, and Joss Ackland and David Burke went through their paces beneath us. For several minutes we had an amazing aerial view and then we crept back unheard and unseen to our own theatre to continue with our own performance.

WHO IS THE REAL KATE O'MARA?

It is said that the adrenalin that is pumped around people's bodies on a first night gives the performance an electrical intensity that is seldom equalled again during a run. This may well be true, but I personally prefer to be more relaxed and on top of the situation, although there is no doubt that there is something addictive in the excitement of the atmosphere.

It is this sort of pressurised situation that I am continually putting myself through, as I do many plays and usually have about three first nights a year, that compels me to find some form of relaxation which is completely unemotional and un-demanding. I am not particularly domesticated, of which more later, but I find that decorating is a great form of relaxation. I love painting – I mean painting walls and ceilings and skirting boards and things. I adore slapping colour on blank surfaces, for I thrive on change and variety. I have a very low boredom threshold and painting rooms a different colour is one way of alleviating this condition. I did briefly go to art school to study theatre design, but alas, as with my piano playing, I had no inspirational talent for it. I can draw or paint almost anything you care to mention, but it is simply a copy. I cannot produce anything of my own, but only reproduce something that someone else has done. However I am extremely happy with a paintbrush in my hand, whether painting rooms or theatrical sets. One of the best things about it, apart from the change one has wrought, is the fact that it is quick – one can see instant results. As the reader may have gathered, I am extremely impatient: everything has to be 'now', and the results of one's labours with a paintpot and brush are instantaneous.

I also enjoy walking, which enables me to take exercise and leaves my mind free to roam elsewhere at the same time. I can walk for miles and for hours, and be completely entertained. I also enjoy driving. Touring does not daunt me, partly because of my ability to adapt to change and the facility I have for making a home quickly and easily wherever I am, and partly because I look forward to the drive to whatever place in the country I am playing. Even if the date is in some unpromising industrial town, the countryside round about these places is nearly always glorious and I map out a route for myself that will enable me to see the best of it. I find somewhere charming to stop for lunch en route, and once again I am able to appreciate my independence and freedom.

One of the things that I missed desperately while I was in California – I think the single reason for my home-sickness – was the seasons. I suppose it is my predilection for change and variety in life that makes the unpredictability and seasonal nature of the English weather so essential to my well-being. Other people – usually British people who are starved of sunshine, year in and year out – long for climes such as those of California. It was one of the first things commented on by the Emperor Augustus when he visited Britain in something like AD44: he was fairly disparaging about the dampness and mist and general sogginess of the atmosphere of the isles of Britain.

What I like about the English weather is you never know what it's going to do next. It's a permanent challenge. Californian sunshine is all very well, but it is predictable and relentless. When you draw back the curtains in the morning there it is every day – cloudless blue skies, burning sun. Even when a pall of smog hangs over the city of Los Angeles, it usually gets burned off during the day by the blazing sun. I think it only rained twice the whole time I was there and I must say the rain was very dramatic – monumental and wonderfully refreshing.

The great thing about the glorious weather in California is that it makes everything dark green and luxuriant. That is, of course, providing you water it religiously every day. When I first moved into my garden apartment in West Hollywood the 'garden' was completely arid. However, thanks to my good friend Jenny Agutter's sound advice, I went and purchased lots of little plants

The launch of The British Actors' Theatre Company. I am being held aloft by Tim and Peter Woodward. (*Solo Syndication*)

The outfit I blew £300 on to do the test for *Dynasty*. (*Joe Bangay*)

With Joan Collins in 1986. (*ABC*)

The *Dynasty* cast, including Joan Collins, John Forsyth and Linda Evans.
(*Scope Features*)

Left: In *The Italian Girl* at Wyndham's Theatre in 1967. It was during this play that I managed to slip out and 'corpse' Paul Schofield, who was appearing next door. (*Anthony Crickmay*)

Right: A typical movie still pose from the Swinging Sixties. (*Monitor Press Agency*)

Losing my temper on screen. The victims are Peter O'Toole and Zero Mostel in *Great Catherine* (1967). (*Warner Bros*)

With co-star Richard Easton off-set, during the making of the TV series *The Brothers* in 1976. (*Jim Monk*)

Left: My first appearance in *Doctor Who* in 1985. I played a character called The Rani and Anthony Ainley played The Master. (*BBC Enterprises*)

Below: The Rani disguised herself as a ninety-year-old woman to lure young male victims into her laboratory for experiments in time travel. (*BBC Enterprises*)

Left: Back again as a rejuvenated Rani in 1987. (*BBC Enterprises*)

Playing a Dumb Blonde in *Light Up The Sky* at the Old Vic in 1985. (*Sun*)

A still from the new series of *Howard's Way* showing me with Stephen Yardley and Susan Gilmore. (*BBC Enterprises*)

Dickon aged seventeen, in 1980. (*Scope Features*)

Right: A 40th birthday photo by my actress friend Sue Brown.

Left: A modelling shot – the finished result after several hours of preparation.
(*Associated Newspapers*)

I played Goneril and Isla Blair was Regan in the 1987 production of *King Lear*. (*John Haynes*)

With the late Sir Anthony Quayle heading his company, Compass, on tour in *King Lear*. I gave up *Dynasty* to do this.

Wooing scene from *The Taming Of The Shrew*, with Tim Woodward. This was The British Actors' Theatre Company's first production, in 1987. (*Mike Martin*)

With Philip Madoc in *Duet for One* in 1982. We toured Britain and Europe. (*Sophie Baker*)

Doing my own makeup for *Cleopatra* in 1979 – my first attempt at the part.

Photo for a poster advertising The British Actors' Theatre Company's production of *Cleopatra* in 1989. (*Joe Bangay*)

A 50th birthday photo taken by Joe Bangay – just a bit of campery to show off my figure.

A 1988 photo by the *News Of The World* – typical tabloid shot!

called Babies' Tears, plus various other sorts of fast-climbing foliage. We planted these Babies' Tears at regular intervals all over the garden and stuck in the climbers near the terracotta walls. We watered these thoroughly, drenched them in fact. Literally within a couple of days they were growing, and within a couple of weeks the garden was completely covered with dark green, verdant loveliness. This complete transformation was brought about entirely by warmth and moisture.

However, in spite of this miracle of nature my soul cried out for the glorious autumnal hues that I had left behind. It was autumn and I could picture only too vividly how stunning the country lanes would be looking. I returned home briefly after my first stint in LA and I remember the shock of joy I experienced when driving back to my home in the country. The trees were almost orange, the atmosphere was dank and damp, and it was like having a wonderful cool clear drink of water after weeks in the desert.

I think it is the evidence of so much life force in England that makes it so attractive. There's always so much happening, even when nature is dying, that one knows full well that it is merely renewing itself. I believe Hollywood in the old days was quite something, a place of orange groves with the scent of their blossom hanging in the air. Sadly these are no longer there. This symbolises one of the facts I find difficult to understand about the Californians: their eternal quest not only for youth but for newness. They don't seem to have any feeling for their history, albeit cinematic history, and don't seem to realise how fascinating it is to the rest of the world. I looked in vain for exotic places I had read about from the early days of Hollywood. They were not to be found. They have been razed to the ground and new buildings erected in their stead. Many of the studios are new and doubtless very well equipped, but I was quite happy to be working in one of the older-style studio lots, in this case the old Goldwyn Studios, now known as Warner Hollywood. They were very reminiscent of Pinewood or Elstree, and therefore reassuringly familiar.

I like things from the past, things that have been part of other people's lives. One of my great pleasures is to set off early in the day with enough money in my purse to go antique hunting. This, of course, is a luxury, but one that I revel in. I am not searching for anything specific, simply something that takes my fancy. I don't go out looking for clothes or shoes or belts or anything to put on me, but I love to find things to put in my home: things that I can look at and cherish, because of their age and beauty. I love old country furniture. It is often not particularly even or well finished, but it invariably has a patina that can only be achieved by years of wear and polish and one can see the craftsmanship that has been lovingly bestowed upon each piece. It was made to be functional, to be used, and this is how I like to treat all my furniture. It is not there to be gazed at in wonder, but to be used by all and sundry.

I like to make my home a place of comfort and warmth, not a cold, unwelcoming museum. Once I have found my antique, I spend the rest of the day rearranging the articles already in my house to accommodate the newcomer. I love rearranging the furniture – yet another manifestation of my passion for change. I change the colours of the walls, I make new curtains, and I change the look of the room by altering the furniture around.

A man I once lived with used to say he often thought he'd come home to the wrong place because when he walked through the front door he didn't recognise anything. Of course they were the same pieces of furniture. It's just that I had rearranged them in order to achieve exactly this effect, to make it look completely different. But men don't like change; they like the familiar. Change on the whole seems to unsettle them, and I must say that, even though I am always on the move, when I have been away from my home for any length of time it is a great joy to get back to my familiar nest.

WHO IS THE REAL KATE O'MARA?

My other pleasures in life are few, and I think remarkably simple. A great delight to me is to curl up alone in a huge double bed with an electric blanket, Radio 3 playing quietly in the background and the *Observer* crossword in front of me. When I am bored with that or have finished it, I like to fall asleep over a good book. To me this is the height of indulgence since I spend nearly every night of my life on stage, apart from brief gaps for Christmas and Easter, and the odd Sunday here and there. Such indolence is wonderfully sybaritic.

I seldom go to the cinema, but I love watching movies on television. The trouble with going to the cinema for me is that I am often recognised, which makes life very difficult. And there is something wonderfully luxurious about seeing movies in one's own home, as though one had one's own private cinema. So after the movie it's off to bed in the electric blanket with the crossword followed by the book, again to the accompaniment of some beautiful music, and then off to sleep.

These things would make an ideal day for me if I were on my own, but if I were accompanied by the man of my choice it would be slightly different. Instead of tracking down antiques we would go to some place of historical interest and have lunch in a wonderful coaching inn (alone, I would plump for a vegetarian restaurant or pass up lunch altogether). The afternoon would be devoted to a massive walk in the countryside and in the evening we would get dressed up to go out to the theatre. Preferably it would be part of a weekend away. I love weekends spent with a man when there is no washing up to do and one can just wander around and explore new places and dress up and dine out. It is all fearfully indulgent, I know, but I can honestly claim that I work very hard to earn such treats.

Talking of treats, there are several in my life. Because I exist on a strict diet (see Chapter 6) I do find it quite wonderful about every six months to go into a café and order a plate of egg and chips. After my unrelenting diet of avocados and salads it is extremely stimulating. I don't feel the least bit wicked when I've done it – I really feel I have deserved it. As I neither drink nor smoke, these little lapses are, I think, essential.

I say that I don't drink, and that's true, but there are occasions when I can be persuaded to gulp down some well-watered whisky if, for example, I have had a shock or there has been an unpleasant emotional incident, usually connected with the incursions of the press. I invariably regret it. No matter how small the intake of alcohol, the resulting headache is gargantuan and the depression monumental. Whenever I am with someone for any length of time one of my first instructions to them is 'For God's sake, don't let me drink, not even the tiniest amount.' At first of course they don't believe me and long for me to join them in their libations, but soon they learn otherwise and and agree reluctantly to abide by my instructions.

I have never smoked in my life. This is not some wonderfully puritanical stance that I have adopted, but simply a means of attracting attention to myself at a very early age. By being the only person in my group who wasn't smoking I immediately became an object of intense interest, if only by having the willpower and apparent self-confidence not to follow the herd. It was all an act, of course, and rooted in deep insecurity. But I have always found the best method of defence to be attack.

I am now very glad that I don't smoke, but I do have one addiction, which is tea. I cannot manage without it, ever. I have tried, but to no avail. Nor, as I've already said, can I manage without sugar in tea. This is a heinous crime, I realise, but it is one of my many weaknesses and I admit to it freely.

Despite being a girl of simple tastes – tea is hardly the kind of addiction you would connect with fast living – there have been times in my life when I have found myself among the 'beautiful people', or the 'jet set' as we used to call them in my heyday. I can cope, but I am not entirely at ease in their company. It is fun for a while, if only to see how the other half lives and loves, but I prefer the simple life. That is why the world of the movies and television doesn't really appeal to me all that much. There seems to be an attendant lifestyle with these two particular aspects of the entertainment industry with which I do not empathise, although it can be amusing for a very short while. In the past I have been to the Cannes Film Festival, for example when one of my films was being shown there. I have tested for movies at Cinecittà in Rome and lived it up on the Via Veneto. I have been seen round swimming pools in the South of France and of course in Beverly Hills, but these are isolated incidents in my life. I am glad to have had these experiences, but they are not ones that I would care to repeat too often.

This is one of the many reasons why I am happier working in the theatre, where such extravagant behaviour is not expected of one. I think in the old days it might have been, but now it is perfectly acceptable to play Cleopatra on stage and then come home and potter about the garden, tying up rosebushes and gathering wild blackberries to make one's own jam. I remember one year I concocted a most extraordinary wild jam which I christened Hedgerow Jelly. I was playing Titania in *A Midsummer Night's Dream* at the time and was asked to contribute some home produce to the annual gala to raise money for the theatre. I decided to invent something pertinent to the drama in hand and mixed all sorts of fruits to achieve the desired result. The ingredients were wild blackberries, fallen apples, the odd raspberry and strawberry, not to mention blackcurrants and redcurrants, all chucked in together.

I was born under the sign of Leo, and my ruler is supposed to be the Sun. As a lover of the countryside I like the sun very much. I find it optimistic and cheering, it creates pretty dappled patterns in woodland clearings, and generally makes the world seem a better place. But there are times when it is hard to live up to a really beautiful, bright, shining day. It is sometimes difficult to know how to cope with a really glorious hot afternoon. My way is to collapse in a heap and endeavour to get a suntan. If I am indoors and working, or playing a matinee audience to a half-empty theatre, I simply, as I've mentioned before, have to put it out of my mind.

The days that really turn me on, are dark, dank, overcast and grey. I love lowering clouds. I love the smell of rain and the earth after a summer shower. I love it when the world is overhung with a thick grey mist. I think it is because I feel I have to rise to the challenge, to make something of such a day. It seems dark and mysterious and in some way I may be able to brighten it up. It is possible that, because the sun is a propagator of life, I feel that I am somehow borrowing time. That when the sun does not shine, maybe time has stood still and one has been granted a brief respite and another day of life. There is something about the sounds on such a day. They seem clearer and more resonant, and it is as though one can hear down the ages and touch another time altogether – particularly, of course, in the country-side. I feel one can have magical experiences on such days.

I like to think however, that I am not too superstitious. Contrary to theatrical lore I mention the name *Macbeth* frequently and have even been known to quote from it on occasion without batting an eyelid. But I avoid walking under ladders, and I flinch visibly when I see one magpie, after which I feel depressed for the rest of the morning. I am overjoyed when I see two and immediately feel confident that everything is going to be all right.

I seem to possess many of the virtues, faults and characteristics attributed by astrologers to Leos. Whether this is because I am naturally so or, being aware of these attributes, I try to encourage them, I cannot say. But the fact of the matter is that I am proud, arrogant, a leader, generous (I hope), an exhibitionist, dramatic, theatrical and extrovert in every possible way. I imagine that my rightful place is on the throne and that everyone should acknowledge my authority. However, by way of contrast I am also shy, retiring, gentle, home-loving, and all the things that are the opposite of what I have just described. This, I am led to believe, is because my rising sign is Cancer.

Make of this what you will. I think it is amusing and diverting and gives one endless hours of innocent pleasure and speculation. I occasionally read my stars in one of the many newspapers that feature them, and quite often they are accurate. And quite often they are not. But they are fun, and I think that is probably the most sensible way to regard them.

The other thing that I am supersititous about is peacock feathers. It is idiotic, I know, but I will not have a peacock feather in the house. It is a great shame because they are utterly beautiful, but the only two occasions in my life when I have deliberately acquired them and had them in my abode have been times when events of a cataclysmic nature have ensued. So I have abandoned the peacock feathers and I am still trying to be friendly with magpies!

I have been told by many of my friends that I have the life force, by which I think they mean I have an unbounded supply of nervous energy. This is very useful, because it gets things done and I can go on working for hours without getting tired. People on the whole find it very attractive. It means I bound in and out of people's lives, hopefully brighten them up for a while, and then leap off in another direction.

However, like most things in life, something as positive as this has its negative side as well. I refer of course to my temper. My temperament. My artistic temperament. Or at least that is how I like to think of it. It's all an excuse, of course, to justify the appalling volcano inside me that erupts from time to time. The ghastly thing is that the more I try to control it the worse it gets. It has been the bane of my life and has destroyed many of my relationships. Men simply can't take it, and I really cannot blame them. It is an alarming spectacle.

People who know me well have come to regard it as a sort of

cabaret performance. If Peter Woodward, my co-director and co-founder of the British Actors' Theatre Company, doesn't happen to be in the show that we are working on, he will turn up at a rehearsal and enquire in a pleasant way: 'Has Kate lost her rag yet?' If the reply is in the negative he will grin from ear to ear and say, 'Oh boy, you don't know what you're in for.' If the reply is in the affirmative, he'll say, 'Oh, bugger, I'm sorry I missed it.'

I remember one particular time, when I was raging around the room like a tornado, I was stopped dead in my tracks by observing my audience of fellow actors in the rehearsal room all gazing at me and smiling. So it seems quite obvious to me that they don't take it seriously at all. In a way I find this comforting, because my temper distresses me greatly. I find it deeply disturbing that I seem to have no control over this hideous explosion that lurks inside me, waiting for an opportunity to be let out.

It manifests itself in any number of ways, quite often in self-abuse. If I am rehearsing a stage play and forget my lines in the middle of a scene, I swear roundly a great deal and, if I continue to dry, start hitting myself. The one thing to be said in my defence is that it is always myself whom I hit. I am not given to hitting other actors, except when the action of the play demands it.

There is, however, one notable exception to this! I once beat up an actor on stage, in the middle of a performance. The unsuspecting audience that night were completely unaware that they were witnessing a real-life drama. I had had a rather traumatic time with my leading man on this occasion and we had had some fairly hairy rows. We were playing opposite each other in *The Taming of the Shrew*, a play that involves a certain amount of physical knockabout 'fun' between the leading protagonists. That is if one is doing a reasonably traditional production. We were.

WHO IS THE REAL KATE O'MARA?

On making my entrance into our first meeting in the play, my Elizabethan dress caught on a nail as I was coming through the door. This prevented me getting on stage and starting the scene in the usual way. Now one of the most exciting things about appearing in the theatre is that the performance is different every night. This can happen because of the mood of the audience, the mood of your fellow actors, the amount of energy that is being pushed out from the actors to the audience (hopefully recharged and shoved back again from the audience to the actors), and any number of intangible elements. One of these intangibles is when something goes wrong, which always provides an added *frisson* to the events because the actors have to busk their way around it, improvising madly.

So I tried to get through the door, found my dress caught on a nail and had to get out again and try to come in again. But the dress was so firmly lodged on this nail that I was simply rooted to the spot. I tried with such force and vehemence – in character, of course – that I sat down rather abruptly. As Katherina, the Shrew, is at the beginning of the play a very forceful, aggressive woman, this was all grist to the mill. I did a lot of Katherina-type acting of being furious that I had made an ungainly impression on my would-be suitor, who was standing on stage at the time. To my dismay he just stood there and watched me. I felt that he should have taken advantage of the moment and started when I was sitting on the floor, thus making a very splendid comic start to the scene. But this did not happen. With difficulty I got to my feet, tore my dress from the nail, marched on stage and glared at him. Still he did not start the scene. As he had the opening lines it was impossible for me to start it. So I turned my back on him and sat abruptly and determinedly on a nearby bench. This was not the usual action at this point. Finally he started the scene, but for me the moment had passed. I turned and glared ferociously at him and then came in with my lines.

Then we got to the bit where we were supposed to have a sort of cat fight. The events of the day, plus his not taking advantage of the improvised situation, suddenly got to me. Something snapped inside me and I went for him. I mean, I really went for him! This was no stage fight – it started off as one but it continued for real. I hit him, I pounded him, I kicked him, I bashed him, I pushed him, I shoved him, I did everything I could. It went on and on. Every time my eye glanced towards either of the wings, I saw that they were gradually filling up with actors who realised that something good and unrehearsed was happening on stage. By the end of the scene the wings were packed, and people were standing on chairs trying to get a better view. My leading actor and I were completely winded, were both on our knees unable to breathe or continue with the scene. This is what I call real live theatre.

My temperamental activities are not, however, restricted to the live theatre. I have been known to lose control in real life as well. I vividly remember one occasion when my then boyfriend sent me out to buy a cake for tea. I am not a great cake fan, in fact I don't really like cakes at all. But he wanted a cake, so being, as I have mentioned before by way of contrast, a rather affable creature, off I went. It was late on Saturday, so the shops didn't have much left, but I managed to come back with a coffee cream sponge. It was quite beautiful in its own way, all sort of puffy and light and fluffy – one of those really gungy ones. I remember him ambling into the kitchen and saying, 'Oh, I don't like coffee cream cakes', and strolling out again. As I had gone to five different shops and on a bicycle to boot to obtain this piece of goo, I was more than irritated. I was absolutely furious. I picked up the cake in my right hand, followed him into the living room and with a deadly aim plus the force of Fatima Whitbread hurled the offending article straight at him. He turned just in time to see it hurtling towards him, and ducked. It ricocheted off the opposite wall and splattered over the entire room. Although it took hours to clean the place up (indeed I was still finding little bits and pieces of dried stale coffee sponge crumbs for weeks afterwards) it was nonetheless one of the most satisfying experiences of my whole life.

I used to pick fights with men in youth, but I haven't done this for some time because of course one is bound to lose. But in my time I have belaboured men with various pieces of kitchen impedimenta, household artefacts and stage props. I have nearly always come off worst.

I wonder when my temper will cease to torment me. Will it ever go away? I was hoping that I would mellow with the years, but to my dismay I seem to be getting worse. Of course the nervous energy that gives rise to it all means I am able to do about five things at once and usually do. At the time of writing this I am filming *Howard's Way*, rehearsing a stage play of which I am also the producer and financier, setting up three other theatre productions, and working on a Shakespeare Workshop production to be filmed. Even a temper like mine has its compensations!

Going to the other extreme of personality traits, my mother has been heard to say that a little charm goes a long way. I know she is right. Charm makes life more pleasant for the person on the receiving end, and it is one of the methods I employ when endeavouring to get my own way in any situation, usually one of conflict. I start by using charm, then I become more forceful and determined, and finally I resort to blackmail. But it is much better to get what one wants by charm, and I smile a great deal at people I hardly know in an attempt to win them over. It is twice as difficult for me, of course, because being a femme fatale, I have to work twice as hard.

I too am won over by charm and find it irresistible. I am a complete sucker for flattery of any sort. I respond very warmly to anyone who tells me I am either good-looking or have given a good performance. I warm to them immediately. It's obvious, I know, but I suppose it's very human to do so.

In my capacity as manager and co-director of my theatre company, I am obliged to interview many actors for the various plays we are putting on and I have to sit through many casting sessions. One hates having to sit in judgememt on one's fellow actors, but we have found no other method of gauging whether a person is right for a part if we are not familiar with his or her work. The actor or actress who bounds in with a great deal of charm and enthusiasm, or at least appears to want to work for one and seems pleased to make one's acquaintance, stands a better chance of getting the job. Of course ability is the first thing we are looking for, but if it is a toss-up between two equally able actors one is inclined to plump for the one who is charming rather than the one who is surly.

The main thing about getting one's own way is determination, a complete and utter confidence in what one is doing. I am not good at compromise, although I have been forced to do so on many occasions. And winning a particular argument or getting one's own way after a long, hard battle can sometimes become a Pyrrhic victory. There is sometimes a greater victory to be gained by giving in gracefully.

I think part of my problem is that I suspect I am a tyrant; I am power-mad – that Leo temperament again! I expect my word to be regarded as law and obeyed instantly, and if it isn't I get absolutely hopping mad. Not only mad, but incredulous. It never occurs to me that anyone is going to disagree with me or flout my will. Where I get this from I have no idea, but it can come in useful when running the theatre company, and of course it can make me unpopular. I think I'm too old to change now. I have had various nicknames in my time, among them Her Majesty, Field Marshal O'Mara, Dame O'Mara or Dame O'M, Madam and Attila the Hun. As a baby I was known as Queen Victoria and would hold court in my high chair; my mother informs me – although I confess I have no recollection of this – that people would back out of my presence in deference to my all too obvious authority and superiority. Machiavelli states that it is better for a prince to be feared than loved, and Charmian advises Cleopatra on her harsh treatment of Antony, 'In time we hate that which we often fear.' This may be true, but the fact is that it doesn't disturb me unduly that I am the woman they love to hate. I take a perverse pleasure in inspiring awe and loathing. It is the power, I think, that attracts me.

The tyrant is a side of me that my fellow members in the acting profession see. The public, or at any rate those outside my professional world, are expecting to find something else. There are occasions when I am obliged to make personal public appearances. I dread these. Any terrifying first night in the West End in front of one's peers and a host of critics is better than having to make a personal appearance as 'oneself'. People are always surprised when they meet me and find that I am nothing like they imagined. To enter a room full of staring faces, some of whom are laughing or sniggering in an unnecessarily smug manner or openly hostile, knowing that one is expected to be devastatingly witty and knowing that every woman in that room is examining one in minute detail, is unnerving indeed. Somehow one has to win this particular group of people over to one's side and I find I am forced to do this by making some self-deprecatory remark. If whatever I am saying is greeted with any enthusiasm at all and hopefully a couple of laughs, I feel I have triumphed in a way that I seldom achieve on stage. I am far more nervous when doing one of these appearances than I ever am in the theatre.

The speech is nearly always followed by a chance to meet the members of the public and sign autographs. Some people are charming, some say they never watch the programme I'm in, and some say they've never heard of me but they might as well have my autograph anyway. It is a thoroughly humiliating experience and one I try not to repeat too often. Quite a lot of people seem to think that I am Jackie Collins – would that I were!

Quite a few others are under the impression that my name is O'Hara. As a result this has become a nickname that many of my fellow actors call me by. I find it rather endearing. Otherwise I am known as O'Mara or KOM.

If I feel I am looking good, I can cope with personal appearances much more easily; I then feel that I am not disappointing my public. This depends on so many things. It means that I have to step straight into a car the moment I leave my front door, and do the opposite at the other end. But on countless occasions it has been pouring with rain, or there has been a howling gale blowing, and I have had to find somewhere to restore my equilibrium. This of course doesn't happen in Hollywood, where the weather is permanently fine and one can be sure of turning up for a 'do' looking glorious. But England is a different matter. I often solve the problem by attempting to arrive incognito with my hair loosely pinned under a scarf, wearing dark glasses and an all-enveloping coat or cloak. I then repair to a ladies' loo somewhere and effect a transformation, to the general astonishment of all and sundry.

I remember doing this when I arrived somewhere at the back of Wardour Street to test for *Dynasty*. It was pouring with rain and I turned up completely shrouded from head to foot. The receptionist, an averagely pretty young girl, regarded me with deep contempt and obviously thought nothing of my chances. She gestured towards the ladies' room in a bored manner, plainly thinking that the whole thing was a waste of time. I emerged ten minutes later a veritable butterfly from my previous chrysalis state. She reeled in disbelief at this transmogrification and regarded me with new respect. Thus encouraged by her reaction, I went in and got the job. Little does she realise that she was instrumental in boosting my confidence at that moment!

It will be crystal-clear by now that I do not like making personal appearances. I hate having to be me. I suppose really that is why I am an actress: I prefer to assume the identities of other people. I avoid chat shows and quiz games and panel games like the plague. Of course I am obliged to do a certain amount of work to publicise my theatre company. This I do with a good grace, but reluctantly.

I have virtually no private life. For some reason the tabloids seem inordinately interested in my very personal affairs. Publicity is one of the least pleasant aspects of being an actress. It comes with the job, they say; certainly when one signs a contract one is aware that a certain amount of exposure is demanded of one. I have become used to the lunacy to which I have been subjected in the gutter press for many years now. The stuff they print about one is nearly always salacious, pernicious, vicious and totally inaccurate. I cannot express enough my loathing of those who fabricate such filth. However, I grit my teeth whenever confronted by them and endeavour to put on a brave front and give them more or less what they want.

To my dismay and great shame, the women are the worst. With a few notable exceptions – namely Jean Rook, who has been utterly wonderful to me over the years, and a few others – I fear I cannot accept that we are all sisters under the skin. I like to excuse them by saying that they are of course working for their male bosses and in a male-dominated profession, and therefore have to fight harder. I often wonder if they sleep comfortably at night. They have attempted to destroy my life on more than one occasion, but somehow I have survived these assassination attempts.

I suppose because we no longer have public executions, this garish and obscene display in the Sunday newspapers is the next best thing. My only consolation is that the following day the offending articles are where they belong, at the bottom of somebody's rubbish bin. Perhaps it is unjust of me to condemn them with so much vitriol. Presumably if it didn't sell newspapers, they wouldn't write such garbage. Part of my trouble is that I have always been a rebel, an outlaw – I love to shock, to show my total contempt for this sad, grasping little society in which I live. So since the tabloids like to see themselves as the moral guardians of the people I am often one of their chief targets. I have been a fighter all my life. I think I'm almost happier with my back to the wall and a broadsword in my hand defending myself against the invaders. I would have probably been happier as a man . . . but I digress. And if I had been a man, I would have missed out on those relationships and experiences that, whether fulfilling or not, have been an important part of my life.

4

The Men In My Life

My dealings with the opposite sex have been so singularly unsuccessful that I feel I am not really qualified to speak with certainty on anything to do with men. However, it has come to my notice in my emotionally checkered life that they are in almost every sense contrary. This is a fault usually attributed to women, but in my experience it is men who never react in the way one anticipates.

If, after a first encounter, one is expecting never to see them again, they invariably turn up the next day. A cardinal rule when dealing with them is to pretend that Alexander Graham Bell never existed: one must either unplug all the telephones in the house or hide them in the airing cupboard, under the bed, beneath a mound of cushions or in the washing machine. All these are really very good hiding places except of course when people are trying to make incoming calls – then I can't remember where I have put the phones and go nearly demented trying to find the damn things. But come hell or high water, one must never phone them. Men, that is. Ever. The great thing to remember is that once one has met the Greek god of one's dreams (on the Greek god of mine, more anon), one must instantly dismiss him from one's mind – pretend that he simply does not exist.

Greek gods come in all shapes and sizes, but that matters not a jot. It is often the most unattractive ones, those verging on the gargoylesque, who prove to be the most difficult. Handsome is as handsome does, and they quite often are and do. Women spend so much of their lives avoiding handsome men (thinking they are going to be shits) that good-looking men often have quite a thin time of it. Whereas really awful-looking men attract women in the most devastating way. I think ugliness brings out women's maternal instincts: they imagine that these grotesque creatures are unloved and unwanted because of their repellent aspect. In fact they are all having a whale of a time and putting it about like goats, firstly for the very reason that women feel sorry for them, and secondly because, since they are unattractive, they try harder and are often better at it.

Even when the relationship is on quite a firm footing, it is still advisable to let him do the phoning. And indeed the pursuit, whatever form it takes. Men seem to have this primeval urge to hunt, and thousands of years of civilisation and several decades spent slumped in front of the television set surrounded by overflowing ashtrays and empty beer cans have not blunted this instinct. Even after they have incarcerated you in a nest somewhere and have convinced themselves that they are settled, they will cast the odd roving eye around in other directions. The great thing is not to be incarcerated. One can make a great show of pretending to be so, but in reality one must be out and about and casting an eye about oneself. This is a very necessary form of protection in the battle of the sexes. And battle I truly believe it is. Men, or boys as I like to think of them, have always been a closed book to me. I simply do not understand them; it is as though they are from a different planet. There seems to be a natural animosity between me and them. It is so difficult to communicate with them – like cats and dogs. I feel that my hackles rise and I metaphorically spit whenever I see a man – that is, a man who doesn't take to me.

My relationships with the men in my life have on the whole been stormy and tempestuous. There is a phrase that I use every now and again, which I find very helpful. I first heard it many years ago, quoted as something that Roman Polanski is said to have uttered after one of the personal tragedies in his life. It is 'Cancel and proceed.' This may sound very harsh, but I think it is invaluable advice.

A variation on this philosophy was given me by a friend and colleague, the actor Keith Baxter. I was working with him in a play in the West End and at that time was going through yet another emotional trauma. Keith witnessed the full horrors of this experience, watching me night after night playing a dizzy dumb blonde on stage, a full comedy role, then coming off to sit at my dressing room mirror and sob quietly to myself. The two star dressing rooms at the Globe Theatre have an inter-connecting door, and Keith would stand in the doorway between the two rooms and watch me. Finally he could bear it no longer.

'Amputate, darling,' he announced authoritatively. 'It's the only way, amputate.'

I took his advice and it worked. There is no point in continuing to examine and re-examine the pain of a broken love affair. I think it is quite healthy to look at it as dispassionately as possible, because then, hopefully, one can learn from the experience. But having done that once, the only way to survive is to amputate, cancel and proceed.

For some reason, the exact nature of which I have yet to discover, the men that seem to find me attractive also have one other grand passion in their lives, namely sport. This is usually an all-consuming, all-enveloping passion which occupies the greater part of their lives. It is extremely convenient and I can thoroughly recommend it. It means that one has hours of blissful solitude, hours in which to potter about and do one's own thing.

There is nothing more aggravating then having a man under one's feet the whole time. They get in the way dreadfully and lurk about looking hopefully at one like a dog. I am not quite sure what they expect, but I suspect that basically they are in need of attention – a pat on the head or a scratching on the ribs or something of an equally canine affectionate nature. This hovering in doorways and looming at the top of the stairs and lurking in corners and loitering in the middle of the kitchen can really get on one's nerves. So I can thoroughly recommend *l'homme sportif* – so long as one is not subjected to endless hours spent shivering on the touch line or yawning on the boundary at a cricket match, the finer points of which are completely beyond me.

For those not blessed with a sporting companion, I have an alternative answer. Allot them a den, a snuggery, all of their very own, shove them in there with food and drink and a television set, shut the door on them and they are completely happy for days – nay, months. One can talk hours uninterrupted on the phone to one's girlfriends, one's mother, one's agent, the builder, the interior decorators, indeed almost anyone. One could even conduct an illicit affair and they would be none the wiser!

Something which I have learned about men over the years is that they are unbelievably vain – another trait normally laid at the door of women. Admittedly I mainly go around with actors, but my experiences are not entirely confined to this particular group of males. I have always laid great stress on looking absolutely stunning for whatever man I happen to have in my life at the time; unfortunately I have often found, to my chagrin, that not only do men sometimes not notice that I am looking stunning, but the first thing they do when arriving to pick me up for a date is go to the mirror to check how they are looking. This does not alter my attitude; I still dress myself up to the nines, because part of that vanity involves their whole presentation of themselves to the world outside – and that includes the woman who is on their arm.

They are very unpredictable, and one must not expect too much of them. If they say they are going to be back at half past six, one should really not expect them until nine. If they promise faithfully to remember to do something quite vital, one must always expect to remember to do it oneself. I know it's pandering to them, but it seems to be the way of the world and one must simply accept it and them for what they are. Which on the whole is dear, sweet, alien creatures from another planet.

One can learn to get along with them, but I fear one has always got to be fully clad in late sixteenth-century plate armour with preferably an undergarment of chainmail. There should be a broadsword hanging at one's side and a bow with a quiver full of arrows at one's back. Thus armed in what is, after all, tradition-ally male garb, one might embark on a relationship with one of these strange creatures.

Thirty-two and forty-seven are ages at which men are strangely vulnerable, and they have been known to do the most extraordinary things at these times. (I seem to remember Jesus Christ was particularly active at the age of thirty-two and that he died at the age of thirty-three.) The forty-seven bit of course is the famed male menopause, when they suddenly discover that they are headed for their half-century – usually quite a desirable score in the cricket world, but not, alas, in human years. It is a landmark or milestone, I suppose, making them aware of their mortality and therefore desperate to capture anything they think they might have missed before it is too late. I can't in all honesty recommend this age group: they are mad, bad and dangerous to know, and I strongly advise giving them a very wide berth until they have come through it on the other side and are well into their mid-fifties. Then I think they come to their senses again and might prove to be amiable companions.

My advice has always been to treat men as men treat women, but I have come to the conclusion that I take my own maxim too literally. I never flirt – I consider it beneath my dignity to signal to a man in any way that I find him attractive. Not only do I think I am a queen among women, but I also consider men to be my subjects. Therefore it would not be seemly for me to lower myself even to contemplate flirting. If I 'show out' to a man it is because I intend to do something about it. I don't mess about. I don't play games. If I am interested in a man, I 'go for it', to use one of my favourite expressions. I realise that this is not acceptable female behaviour, and it is certainly not feminine – but then I don't think I am a very feminine person. I have no qualms about making the first move, of being the seducer. It is probably because I have played so many *femmes fatales* that I have convinced myself I am practised in the art, and possibly I am also starting to believe my own publicity. It is certainly the way men expect me to behave, and I don't like to disappoint them.

I don't suppose I will ever fathom men and will probably end up alone, even more irritable and autocratic and deeply eccentric. I think when I reach eighty I should like to dye my hair a wonderful shade of purple and float around in strange garments and boots and drive a silver sports car. I have every intention of growing old disgracefully!

For some reason, the men I have encountered in my life have found it necessary to try to demoralise me, to put me in my place, to cut me down to size. I dare say this is salutory and much-needed therapy for me, but sadly it always seems to erode whatever feeling I may have for them. In reality I am desperately vulnerable and insecure; I feel they realise this and expose and exploit my weaknesses.

Perhaps it's because I like to be boss – to pay the bills, organise the household, obtain the mortgage, get the overdraft, order the new cooker, decide on the interior decor, buy the furniture, and place it according to my taste. In other words, I like to be in control. And although *some* men may enjoy this, there must be a great many that resent it bitterly.

I have a horrible feeling, that I go even further than that and probably regard men as a slightly inferior form of life. I have no idea how to treat them. Whatever one does seems to be wrong. If one is nice to them and takes them cups of tea in bed in the morning they take this for granted and expect it all the time – it never seems to occur to them that occasionally it might be nice to return the compliment. If one treats them badly, for example by not phoning them, or not being available when they want you to be, or refusing to fall in with their plans, or not cooking them a meal and most certainly not doing their ironing, this seems to work very well for a time. But the trouble is that I hate to be so ungenerous and unkind. If I am living with someone, and I care about them, I like to do things for them, to make life comfortable for them. I always do the housework, but then I enjoy doing the housework. As I think I have mentioned before, I loathe cooking. But I am even prepared to do that. But of course they don't seem to appreciate it. They abuse these privileges and come to expect them all the time. And then of course one becomes a slave or drudge and this simply will not do.

I seem to spend a great deal of my time and indeed my life with younger men, mainly because men of my own age and older simply do not appreciate me. In the past, men have tended to try to take me over, organise me, tame me or at the very least patronise me. I think this is because they feel it is their duty to do so. They see this raging, wild, eccentric virago and, like Petruchio in *The Taming of the Shrew*, decide they must do something about me. I would much rather they left well alone.

Younger men seem to prefer me the way I am. I suspect this is partly because they are far more interested in themselves than in me – whatever the reason, they let me get on and do my own thing, which is what I like. They are also not set in their ways, so are more able to fit in with my regime. They are usually full of energy and enthusiasm and optimism, which corresponds very nicely with my own approach to life; older men become disillusioned, embittered and world-weary as they find that life doesn't come up to their expectations.

On the whole, I tend to fall for actors, simply because I am with them most of the time and we have a common interest. It is essential to me to be with someone who understands the nature of the job. I like a man who is a voracious reader, appreciates good music and art and has a deep and abiding love of the theatre. Not an easy combination to find, especially when a sense of humour and a healthy sexual appetite are the two main ingredients required. One is more likely to find this happy combination in an actor in his thirties than in someone younger. I don't go for very young men, for the simple reason that they don't have enough to offer me – unless of course they are extremely bright.

Even when I was in my twenties I appreciated the sheer vigour of the younger men. I remember being in Rome on location filming. In the cool of the evening I was wandering along the Via Veneto with my then boyfriend, a very good-looking, talented young actor. We suddenly found that we had left some money in our car which was parked down the road, and we were going to be late for our dinner engagement. 'I'll just dash back and get it,' he exclaimed, and raced off like a Greek athlete. The speed with which he tore away into the distance was quite exhilarating. I do find energy enormously watchable:

it is the first thing I look for in a performance, and a prerequisite for any aspiring actor.

Being with a younger man at my present age gives one the illusion of having recaptured at least some of one's own youth. I use the word 'illusion' advisedly. I don't see myself as being in the driving seat, or in a position of power, or as mentor or teacher. Obviously there are elements of this in the relationship, but I like to think that I am open-minded enough to be able to learn from him as well. People have a tendency to become reactionary and conservative as they get older. I hope I don't, and indeed I think I stand a better chance of being available for new experiences and more able to view life with an unjaundiced eye if I am sharing my life with a younger man.

I am aware of an element of the mother manqué as well, but that doesn't worry me unduly. I have always felt I don't have any maternal instinct – maybe I do after all, and this is how it manifests itself. A final benefit is that a younger man's sexual appetite can easily match my own, and, as the reader will by now have appreciated, this is of enormous importance to me.

I like to think that my experience of life can benefit younger men in some way. One hates to preach, but I try to do it in a subtle way by giving advice rather than being dictatorial. I am a great believer in positive thought. Recently Joan Collins showed me a book which she said had been given to her by Pauline Collins. It was called something like *You Can't Allow Yourself the Luxury of a Single Negative Thought*. That sentiment coincides exactly with my own which I try to pass on to my younger man. I know from experience it is so important to grab each moment as it comes; life is so short, and obviously for me it is getting shorter.

The other precept for a happy life that I have learned by hard experience is to try not to worry about the future. It is a completely pointless exercise since we have absolutely no idea what is going to happen. Things seldom turn out the way we expect. We all have to die some time, some sooner than others, so my advice is go for it now. I remember the words of an ex-boyfriend of mine of whom I was very fond, when I suggested doing something fairly revolutionary.

'But darling, why now?' he said. 'We've got the rest of our lives.'

'No,' I replied, '*this* is the rest of our lives!'

I was right, of course. We didn't have the rest of *our* lives, because now we are both with other people, so we should have done it then. But it is very easy to be wise after the event.

People might easily say that by being with a younger man I am simply trying to replace my son, who is now grown up and left home a long time ago. There may be some truth in this. It is also possible that the younger man is looking for a mother replacement, and finds it in the older woman.

I don't think it is quite that simple. There are a number of young men who find the new, independent, younger woman an alarming prospect. She is so self-confident, not necessarily wanting to fulfil the traditional female role of wife and mother, and wanting her own career before having children. Many young men must find this quite daunting and feel therefore more at ease with an older woman who – dare one say it? – is possibly reminiscent of their mother, and therefore familiar and more comfortable. There is no competition, the relationship is likely to be more stable, and there is virtually no chance of having children, therefore there is less possibility of a permanent emotional tie. Younger men who revel in the companionship of women might find the older woman a very agreeable alternative. It certainly is becoming more fashionable and there has to be a sound, sociological reason for its popularity. I find the younger man invigorating, utterly delightful, challenging, constantly surprising and thought-provoking. He makes me rethink my attitude on many subjects and I can thoroughly recommend him. Even if you are unlucky enough to find one that is arrogant, selfish, thoughtless and vain, you're almost certain to have a good time in bed, if nothing else!

That was the cynic in me speaking. For ages now the other side of me, the romantic side, has had this wonderful fantasy of an ideal man. I see a shadowy figure who seems to be a writer or historian or anthropologist or something along those lines. He seems to spend a lot of time in his own room or study, completely surrounded by books. He is working on some wonderful project, a lifetime project, and I am in some way being supportive and helpful and encouraging. I don't see very much of him because he is so immersed in his work. I am thus left free to follow my own pursuits, but we meet occasionally to exchange ideas and enthusiasm and mutual encouragement. This of course is just a wonderful, impossible dream. But one has to dream sometimes.

On a more mundane level, I have often been asked two things: first, how to get a man, and second, how to keep him. For some reason I am thought to be an expert on these two matters. It has been said, of course, that the way to a man's heart is through his stomach. There may be some truth in this, and I know that men on the whole do find food very important. But there is absolutely no doubt in my mind that sex is the prime motivating factor in their lives. Therefore my answer to both the questions is: 'In bed'. I think if one can keep a man happy in bed, one can keep a man happy. Woman are far more interested in sex that men ever realise. Men just go on about it more, whereas women seldom do, except amongst themselves. This book is really addressed to women whose children have grown up, and who are now finding themselves with a new lease of life – and especially sex life. There is an extraordinary feeling of relief when one realises that there is no longer a danger of becoming pregnant. It relaxes one wonderfully.

I think also that men like to be in congenial surroundings. I have devoted a whole chapter in this book to home-making. This is not entirely for my own benefit. It has been my experience that men actually do appreciate these things, though they never mention them. But even if a *House and Garden*-type home is not feasible, I still think a lot can be done with a little ingenuity – and a great deal of sex.

It has been my sad experience that a lot of men find me attractive because I have a reputation as a sex symbol, and have had for many years. They imagine that, by being with me and being seen in public with me, their sexual reputation will be somehow enhanced. Often they are not interested in me sexually at all, a situation I have found very difficult to cope with. Much as I like them as companions, this is simply not enough for me.

The sexually confident man is surprisingly hard to find. The sexually well-adjusted man is even harder to find. There seems to be a breed of man that needs to prove himself sexually by having a lot of girlfriends or keeping more than one mistress whilst in a permanent relationship. This really shouldn't be necessary, and I think it causes a great deal of unhappiness. The trouble is that most men are too frightened to do anything about it, and continue to lead double lives which must increase their chances of heart attacks and high blood pressure as they are living under considerable stress.

It is also well known, of course, that as they reach the male menopause they begin to fear that their manhood is in some way diminishing; so they start a relentless quest for reassurance that they are still sexually desirable. A lot of women I know have been very hurt by being the victims of this particular male malaise.

Some women find the only way to deal with this situation, whether they are wives or girlfriends, is to turn a blind eye. This is all very stoical and commendable. My method is to take a lover. No turning of the other cheek, if you'll pardon the pun, for me. I am a firm believer in an eye for an eye and a tooth for a tooth – or, in this case, a fuck for a fuck. It usually has the effect of pulling them up quite sharply.

I've said that treating men as they treat women is the only way for me. The trouble is that women let them get away with such appalling behaviour for years on end, and it is very difficult to teach an old dog new tricks. One really has to try to grab them while they're still young enough to learn. No one is perfect, of course, and women, although they are the superior sex, have many failings. But men must learn that they simply cannot continue to indulge themselves in the sort of selfish behaviour to which they have become accustomed for centuries. I think women have been largely to blame for this attitude, and the female of the species has to learn that she must rethink her whole approach to men. She must insist on her freedom and independence, and must not pander to the man's every whim or become a drudge.

I think men are already beginning to view women with a new respect. It is difficult for them to make the transition, but they are learning fast. There is of course a new breed of man to go with the new woman. He is an altogether much nicer, gentler person, and is starting to accept woman as his equal in all things. I have high hopes for the men of the future generations.

In my time I have seduced quite a few men – although not so many as people might suppose – but I wouldn't dream of doing so unless I had seen some sign of encouragement from the man in question. One can easily tell whether they're interested or not by observing the body language. I recommend any book that illustrates body language as a good investment for the predatory woman; it is quite easy to misread signals sometimes, and a handbook of this nature is invaluable if one doesn't wish to make a total fool of oneself.

I am afraid my method of seduction is not very subtle. I believe in the direct approach, partly because it disarms and this is a necessary part of the procedure. Men are usually so taken aback that they acquiesce without a murmur, and seem to find it quite exciting that the woman has taken the initiative. But obviously my approach doesn't appeal to all men, many of whom find it intimidating and indeed emasculating. One of my favourite remarks about my television performances was that 'I had a smile that could de-scale a kettle at fifty paces'! I fear I have this effect on some would-be suitors.

Nevertheless I must have had my successes, or I wouldn't have had the enjoyable sex life that I have had and am still having. My introduction to the subject, however, was less than promising, and might even have put me off for life.

As a young girl, I remember thinking that boys were completely insufferable. I loathed and abhorred them. They seemed so pompous, arrogant, opinionated and generally boorish. I had absolutely no time for them and regarded them with deep contempt. They were, of course, the young male chauvinist pigs of my generation. I didn't become interested in boys until much, much later.

I had my first experience of sex at what today would seem the rather advanced age of eighteen. I was accosted by an extremely good-looking young man who offered to take me to the pictures, which he did. He then said he would walk me home, which he did. Crossing Barnes Common he suddenly forced me to the ground and raped me. I had absolutely no idea what was going on, being completely ignorant of the facts of life. In those days nobody talked about them; they were absolutely unmentionable. Nothing was ever explained to one – one had, for instance, absolutely no idea why one bled month after month, other than it had something to do with procreation. This may be difficult to believe now, in this enlightened age, but I can assure you that at the age of eighteen I had no idea what the word 'fuck' meant.

I have to say my first experience was not pleasant. I decided that it must be better than this, but my subsequent experiences up until the age of twenty-six did not persuade me that it was. The whole thing improved dramatically on 11 April 1966 in Dundee, and has been improving ever since! I subsequently married this man and have to say that even though the marriage was not a success, I shall be eternally grateful to him for educating me sexually. He was essaying the title role in *Macbeth* at the time, which may have something to do with my total disregard for the superstitions traditionally associated with this play!

I like my sex to be Jacobean. It is for this reason that, regardless of the period of house in which I am living, the bedroom will always have a late seventeenth-century flavour to it. It should be full of drapes, curtains, lace pillows, ornate mirrors, candles glowing in dark corners casting strange shadows, heavy dark oak furniture, and hopefully a rather beautiful man. To enjoy sex fully I have to feel that I am looking my very best – preferably stunning. This is why I always try to go to bed wearing rather a lot of make-up and smothered in scent. If I feel I am not looking my best I don't enjoy it so much.

I like men to be romantic in bed. The biggest turn-on is a man in a sort of eighteenth-century white shirt. I like to be stroked and soothed – having one's back stroked is particularly pleasant. Kissing is wonderful, and I prefer the gentle touch. I think the whole thing should be taken very seriously indeed. I am not into jokey or jolly sex – it is no laughing matter. I take my sex seriously and passionately, and expect my lover to do the same.

I think the best thing about love-making is being loved, if only in a physical way. Being hugged and caressed and kissed and stroked is one of the most beautiful feelings in the world. That was what I missed most during my brief spell of celibacy; I have a need to be cherished. Everything seemed very cold and bleak and unloving then. A relationship without sex for me is unthinkable.

I cannot understand why women wear nightdresses, and pyjamas on either sex are simply absurd. I would simply refuse to go to bed with a man who was wearing pyjamas – they look utterly ludicrous. I once remarked to a friend of mine (male) that I could understand a man not liking me, but I couldn't understand a man not fancying me: I regard it almost as a crime. I will only go to bed with good-looking men, preferably handsome ones. It doesn't matter whether they are tall, short, blond or dark, so long as they are pretty. They are usually shits, of course – but then as one never expects anything else, it doesn't matter.

One of the reasons I work so hard at keeping my figure in good shape is because I don't want these pretty, shitty men to be disappointed when they go to bed with me. But most of all I don't want to be disappointed myself. And unless I live up to my own expectations of myself, I will be.

As you may have gathered, sex is all important to me. I don't think I could exist without it. On the few occasions when I have been forced to for one reason or another (usually recovering from yet another disastrous love affair), I have felt desolate. I know full well that however desperate or unhappy I have been over some broken romance, it can always be cured by going to bed with yet another pretty man.

My attitude to relationships may sound very shallow, but I don't think I have ever really met a man who cared deeply about me, or at any rate deeply enough. I suspect this is because they know that I am very self-sufficient, and that, perhaps I can manage without them – that maybe I don't need them. I suppose that's why sex is so important to me. It takes the place of love in my life; or it is the only form of loving that I experience. It is probably why my appearance is so terribly important to me. I don't expect people to love me as a person, for I am not a very lovable woman. I think I am selfish, autocratic, independent, self-opinionated, vain and thoroughly bad-tempered. But I like to think that when I go to bed with someone I become generous, tender, loving, caring, vulnerable and extremely affable. I suppose it is because I have had so many emotional disasters in my life that it is only the physical side of love that I really trust. That at least has been a success, so that is what I always go for.

5

Woman – the Stronger Sex

My experience of my own sex has been on the whole edifying, and there is no doubt in my mind that women are the superior sex. For companionship and friendship and loyalty and compassion I choose my girlfriends every time. They are wonderful. What I would do without them, heaven alone knows. I feel relaxed and easy and comfortable in their company; I feel protective towards them; I feel I can confide in them and they in me. With men I feel tense, uneasy, aggressive and generally uncomfortable. Except in bed of course. Then everything is all right.

Women can be generous to a fault, compassionate, tenacious, stoical, selfless, tough, determined and utterly ruthless. I list all the above as virtues. Just occasionally, however, one comes across a woman who does not deserve the name, and of that more later. The great thing about most women is that under pressure they are at their best. They will behave in a magnanimous manner and show the sort of bravery that a mere man would be proud of.

In many ways, I think women have the advantage in business situations these days. Men have been used to fighting battles for centuries and are familiar with the various strategies and tactics that are employed – by men. But women, being physically weaker, have been obliged to engage in tactics of a different nature: psychological warfare. And I think this is where they have the advantage over men – the age-old, common, well-tried method of the surprise attack.

Men are always complaining that they don't understand women, that women are complicated creatures. There is a certain amount of truth in what men say. I think men are much more straightforward and less devious than women. They have had no need to develop deviousness over the centuries, whereas women have been forced to employ methods of labyrinthine complexity in order to survive.

I think we are on the brink of the dawn of the new age of the supremacy of woman. I hope I am alive to see it flower and burst out in all its glory. It would be sad if womankind reverts to the male-oriented stereotype of submissive woman. Thousands of years of conditioning are hard to eradicate, and we all know that the veneer of civilization is only paper-thin and that *in extremis* man (I use the word in its general sense) will revert to his primeval bestial state, but I live in hope. I suspect that the supremacy of woman may be the salvation of this planet.

I have been told by many men that they are frightened of me. It is awful to think that one inspires fear in any one. But I don't think this is something that is peculiar to me. I think many men are frightened of women – with very good reason. Women, after all, live longer than men. Women are the great survivors. They are the bringers of life. They know the secret of life. They understand about preservation and self-sufficiency and, above all, self-reliance. They have learned the hard way, and there is no better training ground.

But some women are, sadly, not worthy of their sex. The sort of woman I cannot abide is the one who uses her femininity to get her own way; or rather I should say abuses her femininity. The 'little girl' performance makes me want to vomit, especially when it is exhibited in one who has long since attained maturity. Except of course she is not mature in the true sense of the word. The woman who uses her sexuality to get what she wants I have slightly more time for; female sexuality is a lethal weapon which, correctly employed, can be devastating. At least here she is fighting on the same terms as the man.

The woman I have no time for is the one who uses emotional blackmail. I think it is the most degrading form of behaviour and utterly contemptible. I am ashamed that such a woman belongs to the same sex as myself. Worse still is the woman who uses her children to try to hold a man, or deliberately becomes pregnant to try to win him in the first place. I cannot find words that sufficiently express the outrage I feel at such behaviour. I think above all a woman should be dignified. If she finds herself pregnant, it is as much her fault as his, and because she is the one who has to cope she should either get on with it and bring up the child herself, if the man doesn't want to know, or have an abortion.

I realise that what I have just said will provoke a storm of protest. I am not a Christian, I do not believe in God, and I have no religious affiliations or beliefs whatsoever. So far as I am concerned, we are all fellow creatures for a short space of time on this planet; how we got here, or where we go, if anywhere, afterwards, I have not a clue. All we can do is do the best we can while we are on this earth. I think to bring an unwanted baby into an already vastly overcrowded world is possibly a crime.

Moralists who pontificate otherwise are, I am afraid, the victims of thousands of years of sociological conditioning and religious prejudice. It is a ridiculous idea that a family unit is essential to our mutual well-being. This eternal puritanical attitude towards moral behaviour is almost entirely the result of religious bigotry. More harm, more suffering, more pain, more injustice, more human misery, more wholesale slaughter has been perpetrated in the name of religion than almost anything else in the history of the world. And the whole thing is based on fear, because we pathetic little mortals cannot bear the idea that we may simply have come from some sort of primeval slime and will ultimately end up as a handful of dust.

The tyranny of religious belief has also been responsible for the subjugation of women. Even the New Testament teachings of Jesus Christ, enlightened though they are about social equality, do not take sexual equality into account. The current furore about the ordination of women into the Church of England demonstrates most vividly to me that there are seldom people who are more un-Christian in their behaviour than the followers of Christ.

In other respects women are managing to free themselves from their historical and biological chains. Around about the year AD 910 Aethelflaeda of Mercia led an army into battle against the invading Danes. She had left her husband to become a soldier when, after the birth of her daughter, she is said to have refused the nuptial bed, thinking it 'a foolish pleasure that brought with it so grievous a pain'. It is nice to think that over a thousand years ago there were truly liberated women finding an alternative lifestyle to the traditionally accepted and prescribed one.

It has always seemed grossly unfair to me that the cessation of a woman's reproductive cycle manifests itself in physical terms in a frequently unpleasant and uncomfortable way. We have to put up with mess and discomfort every month of our lives from the age of about eleven onwards for the privilege of being able to give birth. Birth itself is an extremely painful and messy business. We have barely recovered from the ordeal when the same boring old monthly cycle starts all over again until the next pregnancy, which makes us unsightly and ungainly for several months. The whole hideous business then proceeds to wind itself down in the shape of hot flushes, headaches, night sweats, general irritability and, worst of all by far, acute depression. The ageing process, which up to that point was proceeding in a sort of fairly gentle manner, suddenly accelerates as though nature had decided that because we are no longer baby-making machines we are virtually redundant. The old crone has long been a nightmare figure and features terrifyingly in fairy stories. For centuries innocent elderly women living alone were hanged or drowned or burnt at the stake as witches. The old maid has been ridiculed, a figure of fun.

There is no doubt in my mind that the liberation of women has been secured with the help of the contraceptive pill and now hormone replacement therapy. They have both helped to free us from the tyranny of our biological circumstances which in turn is enabling us to take our rightful place in society as equals with men.

At the press launch for the British Actors' Theatre Company I was besieged by the press, since it was my first time back in England after going to Hollywood and they seemed astonished by my appearance. I have never made a secret about my age. This is not entirely of my own doing simply because at the age of twenty-six, I was invited to go into one of the many *Who's Who* publications. At such a young age it never occurred to one to tell anything but the truth, and when my date of birth was requested, I wrote it truthfully. Therefore, my age has always been known by anyone who cared to look it up. So, as I say, journalists and photographers alike were aware that I was at the time of the press launch, forty-eight.

I had gone dressed for the press in an outfit I knew they would appreciate. There is absolutely no point in spending money on launching something if nothing is going to appear in the newspapers. The whole idea of publicity is to make people aware of one's presence, and in this case, as we had so little money, it was imperative that the public came to see the show. So I had chosen to wear a black leather mini-skirt to show my legs, topped with a tee-shirt emblazoned with the company name. The assembled journalists said they found it difficult to believe that I was in fact forty-eight. What was I on? queried one. Hormone pills? As a matter of fact I was, I replied, again seeing no reason to lie. What sort? they countered. And so my endorsement of hormone replacement therapy hit the headlines. Since then I have found myself an unwitting champion for this particular aid to the older woman. It was my fellow actress Dinah Sheridan who first introduced me to the benefits of HRT, and indeed we are both featured amongst other of our age on a cassette published by the Amarant Trust. This is a charitable organization set up to make women aware of the benefits of HRT. So many women approaching the change of life have met with a complete lack of understanding by their GPs that it had become imperative to publicise their particular treatment and make it widely available. The organization has done sterling work in this area, overcoming prejudice, giving reassurance, encouragement and real help to women who might otherwise have continued to live in misery.

It is now widely known that the various unpleasant symptoms of the menopause are caused by the falling off of oestrogen levels in the body. By topping up the hormone levels the balance is redressed and the symptoms cease. Of course, nothing can actually stop the ageing process, but HRT certainly seems to slow it down a bit.

WOMAN – THE STRONGER SEX

Sometimes I find it difficult to believe that we are living in a sophisticated, late twentieth-century society. You would have thought by now that, with men landing on the moon and most extraordinary discoveries in outer space, a moderately successful actress's claim to have benefited from the use of HRT would have been accepted without too much excitement. Not a bit of it. I had outraged letters from women's movements claiming that I had made HRT sound like a panacea for all ills. I had never made any such claim. I have always stated unequivocally that my good health relied to a great extent on the fact that I neither drink nor smoke, have been a vegetarian for virtually all my adult life, take exercise regularly, and watch my diet like a hawk.

But of course there are always people who don't want to hear unpleasant facts. I am used to being vilified. My appearance and behaviour have constantly attracted outrageous comment, quite often from my so-called sisters. I put it down to jealousy. I feel sorry for such women and I shall do my damnedest to continue to shock and outrage them the rest of my life. Fortunately I have met many women who are leading truly liberated, successful, happy lives, running their own businesses, having lovers or not as the mood takes them, married or divorced, childless or with an army of children long since grown up, completely at ease with themselves and with men; they would have no time for such small-mindedness and prejudice and they restore one's faith in the female of the species.

I am frequently asked about the difference that HRT has made to my physical well-being and to compare it to the way I was before I started taking it. This is terribly difficult to identify. I was not suffering from the effects of the menopause before I started taking it, other than blinding headaches which have blighted me all my life. I can only say that I feel more fit now than I ever have. Whether this is simply because psychologically I feel more free than I did in the past, or because I am more successful and have been accepted in my chosen profession, or because of the actual physical benefits of HRT, I cannot possibly say. But I certainly feel wonderful, and have not had to endure the usual miseries that women of my age have in the past been obliged to suffer. And I have to say I get very few headaches. If I do get a headache, the cause is usually due to extreme tension, or tiredness, or overwork, or a combination of all three.

The other criticism levelled at me, and a worry for many women, is my apparent irresponsibility in advocating a therapy with possible side-effects. I can only say that I have never claimed to be an expert in this matter which is why I become so angry when the popular press trivialise it in print. It is a serious medical matter and women must find out for themselves the hazards, just as they did with the contraceptive pill, and then make their own decisions. All I am saying is that it works for me. You take a risk every time you get on an aeroplane or a train or in a car or cross the road. We all have to die some time, but for me and for dozens of my friends and hundreds of other women the taking of HRT has improved the quality of life immeasurably. I rest my case.

One by one, the bastions of social acceptability are falling. One of them is marriage, which I think is one of the most anti-social inventions ever perpetrated on the human race. Sadly, I feel it is women who may have been largely responsible for its survival. It is however, hardly their fault, as the legal protection of a man up until now was paradoxically their only means of survival in a hostile, male-dominated world. But things have changed. Women are now in the ascendancy and marriage has become redundant.

To my utter astonishment, young girls today still seem to be in favour of this barbaric institution. God knows why (and as I don't believe in him, he's hardly likely to tell me). The very fact that the divorce rate is so astronomically high must surely indicate that a marital venture of any kind, whether for love or money, is almost certainly doomed to failure. For some reason second marriages seem to have a better chance of survival, which indicates that it would be wiser to refrain from making lifelong vows to a partner until one is considerably older. As marriage was primarily introduced for the procretion of offspring, this makes nonsense of the whole thing anyway.

On the whole, women are starting to realise that the acquisition of a male in order to survive is a sociological myth. I read somewhere that the happiest women are those that are single, and the happiest men are those that are married; while the unhappiest men are those that are single, and the unhappiest women are those that are married. I am not sure how one resolves this dilemma other than by compromise: in other words, living together. That way each person retains his or her own identity, independence and freedom, and is not riven with guilt if things should not work out.

And as for children, better by far that they are loved and cared for by two separate happy people than trapped in an atmosphere of dull hatred and resentment or, worse still, living with a couple that are tearing each other to shreds. Life is not easy, and it is harder for some than others. And sadly it is a well-known fact that children who have had a sublimely happy childhood in the conventional sense often find it much harder to adjust to the harsh realities of adult life than do those whose experiences in childhood were checkered. Of course, one doesn't wish an unhappy childhood on anyone, but I think our perceptions of what is happy or unhappy are sometimes misconceived. My definition of an unhappy childhood would be one where there is physical, sexual or mental abuse of the child. The everyday rough and tumble of normal life with all its vicissitudes, pain and discomfort has to be experienced from a very early age; the sooner the better I think – then the child has a chance of growing up with a balanced view of the world.

Since I have spent the greater part of my life as an outlaw and rebel, the traditional female roles of wife and mother are not ones that sit easily on my shoulders. Clearly the married state is not for me – the degree of compromise required by one of the parties is daunting indeed, and it would seem that one half of the couple has to go under. I know couples who have succeeded and I am overjoyed for them. I too have tried it, but failed. I suppose I value my independence too much, and I am not prepared to compromise. Many people would call it selfishness, but we are such a long time dead that I feel we must make the most of living, and that for me means retaining my freedom and being single.

Relationships, however, I plunge into headlong without giving a second thought. I like living in the fast lane. This way, of course, I have terrible emotional crashes quite frequently, but I always manage to patch myself up again and hurtle off towards the next one. This has become a way of life with me now, and I can't see it changing.

One of the advantages of not having a permanent long-running relationship is that when it all disintegrates one is more easily able to cope. It is always painful of course, but one finds a way of coping. Work is the greatest therapy of all. I originally wanted to call this book *Survival Kit*, because that is precisely what writing has been to me in the past: a way of surviving. I have often found that putting my thoughts down on paper somehow clarifies them and makes me face them. Actually to see them written makes me come to terms with what I am feeling at the time, however ghastly. And having confronted them, examined them from every possible angle, I am then able to discard them. As I get older the process doesn't exactly get easier; it's just that I get used to it.

I am practised in the art of surviving an emotional catastrophe. I don't really trust happiness. I almost welcome the familiar pain which turns up like an old friend when one has to admit to oneself that a particular entanglement is over. I feel the pain starting to gnaw inside me and I greet it with relief. At least now, I think to myself, I know what to do. I know how to cope with it. I've been here so many times before. Recently it got to the point when I was obliged to stop completely and take stock of myself and my life. I decided that the reasons for all the disastrous encounters I had had with the opposite sex must have something to do with me. I was the common denominator. So I decided to give celibacy a go.

I had tried it before, but on a previous occasion it was an enforced abstinence because I was away from my then boyfriend and wanted to remain faithful to him. However, recently it was a considered decision. I needed to give myself a breathing space, to try to work out what I really wanted and why I was subconsciously always getting myself involved with the most unlikely men. I came to the conclusion that maybe I didn't want a long-term partnership, a kind of marriage; maybe I was frightened of losing my hard-won freedom. Maybe I was just too selfish.

I hated every moment of my enforced chastity, and I am now very thankful that it is over. I have now decided to live my emotional life on a day-to-day basis. I suspect my expectations in the past were always impossibly high and that somehow I had to break the pattern. I don't like compromise, but I guess that is what I have to learn to do.

Having given marriage the thumbs-down, neither have I ever been one of those women who drools over babies and small infants. I don't ever remember feeling broody. I never wanted to have any children. I have never changed my mind over the years, and I am extremely relieved that my child-bearing years are more or less over. However, in spite of these unnatural feelings I have to say that the best thing that has ever happened to me was the birth of my son, Dickon, who is now in his late twenties. He was an enchanting child, became a ghastly adolescent, and is now a delightful adult. I am utterly devoted to him, as I believe he is to me.

Despite the fact that I have been and indeed still am a mother, I am not sure if I am qualified to speak about the *concept* of motherhood. Among my stage roles I have played mothers such as Cleopatra and Lady Macbeth, neither of whom would qualify for the Good Housekeeping seal of approval. I am not quite in this league in real life but I think I must be approaching it, because one well-known attempt employed by my sister to discipline her children was: 'If you don't behave yourself I'll send you to stay with your Aunt Kate'! I am a great believer in discipline, both self-imposed and imposed on other people. I think children in particular benefit from it. I believe it reassures them, makes them feel safe; something to do with order out of chaos, I suppose.

I am sure that one of the reasons children are 'naughty' is simply that they are bored. I can't abide people who patronise children or talk down to them. When my son was small I devised a way of firing his imagination. When I read to him, before he was able to read for himself, I would always choose a book that was slightly beyond his years. He became quite enthralled, and was in a tremendous rush to learn to read so that he could read them all over again for himself. I employed this method for a number of years, with the result that he is still one of the most voracious readers I know. He consumes books all hours of the day and night. I believe it is one of the greatest pleasures in his life. The great thing about children enjoying reading is that it is the complete solitary relaxation. It means that they will sit for hours with their heads in a book and leave one to get on with one's own life.

I was twenty-three when I had my child, but I was not prepared for the experience as this was in the days when nobody talked about anything to do with reproduction. Also there was a firm masculine belief that women were meant to suffer; yet another way of keeping them in their place – subservient to men.

The whole experience of childbirth I found to be like the worst excesses of the Spanish Inquisition. I was totally unprepared for the appalling pain. Of course I had seen countless childbirth scenes in movies, but they were always in Victorian dramas, when, I assumed, things were much worse. How wrong I was.

My son was born on 3 January. It was bitterly cold and I was lying on top of the bed without any coverings. I was lucky to have only a short labour. I am convinced that is because I have very strong stomach muscles and was doing everything I could to push him out. During those six hours, which by most standards is not long at all, I did everything I could to get myself off the bed and over to the window, which I was utterly determined to throw myself out of. I knew that this was the only way I could end this insupportable agony.

I am afraid I screamed the place down. At one point during this ordeal a nurse came into my room and started hitting my legs, saying that I was making an awful lot of noise. I tried to tell her that I couldn't help it, but was unable to get the words out. She came back about half an hour later with a small container of some liquid and told me to take it. She left it on the locker by the side of the bed, where I was completely unable to reach it. I tried several times to turn myself over to get it and failed. I had no idea what the stuff was, but I assumed it was some form of painkiller. However, it was no use to me as I couldn't get at it.

Eventually I found the bell press to summon help. I started pressing it, as I could feel that things were definitely moving apace down below. Nothing happened for ages. I continued to pres the bell and eventually the same nurse reappeared. She was very rough with me again, but I understood why: I think it distressed her to see someone in a great deal of pain, and this was her way of overcoming her feelings. I tried to tell her that I thought the baby was trying to get out, but she simply retorted, 'Nonsense, you've got hours yet!' Feebly I protested that I was sure that I was about to give birth. Finally she had a look and exclaimed: 'Oh my goodness, I can see its head!'

She rushed off to get a wheelchair and with great difficulty got me into it. I was therefore sitting on my son's head all the way down the corridor into the delivery room – he doesn't seem to be any the worse for it, however. I was then manoeuvred on to the delivery bed, while she went off in search of assistance. It being lunchtime, there was absolutely no one around. She kept darting back in to see me, issuing commands which mainly consisted of: 'Don't push!', and then dashed out again to try to find someone. She finally grabbed a passing student doctor who was commandeered to deliver his first baby just as he was on his way to his lunch. I was again exhorted not to push, but it was quite impossible. My son was determined to get out, and the sooner the better.

The pain was so intense that I didn't feel them cut me to ease his entry into the world. After the wonderful relief of the last of him slipping out and the cessation of the pain, I didn't care when they stitched me up again. 'This may hurt,' the young student said. So far as I was concerned, nothing would ever hurt again. There was a good moment when he was cutting the umbilical cord. 'What on earth are you doing?' shrieked the nurse. 'You can't cut it there!' There was a brief hiatus as he reconsidered the situation. 'Oh, come on, give it to me,' she exclaimed irritably, and snatched the instrument away from him and did it herself.

I was then allowed to hold my son briefly. He appeared to gaze up at me in total bewilderment as if to say, 'My God, what have I been landed with!' Then they took him away to weigh him and measure him and clean him up and I was left on my own in the delivery room. I don't think I have ever been so happy in my life. The only way I had of expressing it was to sing. And I sang uninterrupted for about twenty minutes, until they came to wheel me into the general ward.

My arrival was met by a dozen pairs of curious female eyes. One friendly girl asked me what I had had, and then when I told her she said, 'You were the one making all the noise, weren't you?' I don't think I have ever been so ashamed. I looked at all these ordinary women, who presumably had clenched their fists, gritted their teeth and endured their labour in stoical silence. I tried to laugh it off, but I couldn't rid myself of the feeling that I too should have been brave. Such was the propaganda of the myth of childbirth in those days. Thank God things have changed. What the hell does it matter if you make a noise? If it's going to help, scream the place down!

Life in the ward was very regimented. You were only allowed to hold your baby at certain times, feed him at certain times, wind him on command and put him to sleep as regular as clockwork. I used to count the minutes till the next time I was allowed to cuddle him, and I used to spend the whole day gazing in adoration at the little creature in the bassinet beside me. He was unquestionably the most beautiful baby I had ever seen, but of course all mothers say this. He has, however, turned into the most beautiful young man, so I think I had some justification.

The worst thing about the post-natal period, as any mother will tell you, is the lengthy time in which the stitches take to heal. There is no way one can get comfortable as it is impossible to sit on one's bum, so one has to lie on one's side, but turning over is agony. It seems so extraordinary that at the one time when one needs all one's strength and energy to cope with a vigorous new life, one's body is exhausted and feels as though it has been subjected to the most excruciating medieval torture imaginable.

Having once had the experience, why any woman should want to put herself through this unspeakable ordeal again is beyond me. Some women seem to thrive on it – the earth mothers, I suppose. I am probably too selfish. When my son was very small, I made a conscious decision to put him before my career. I have never regretted this, although it has altered the path my career has taken. I would turn down work which would have taken me away from home or was not so financially rewarding. This meant doing the more commercially viable and less artistically worthy jobs and is, I fear, one of the reasons for my glamorous image.

One thing I am extremely grateful to the nursing staff for is their absolute insistence that we all did our stomach muscle exercises to get our figures back in shape. I am sure you will not be surprised to hear that I did them morning, noon and night, as I was determined to get my flat little tummy back again, as soon as possible. I am happy to say my flat little tummy is still with me. And just in case anyone thinks that it is because I was young and supple at the time, my sister had her third child by Caesarian section at the age of forty and by dint of sheer bloody-minded determination also has a nice little flat tummy.

The other really awful thing about the early post-natal period is the notorious four-hourly feeding. Whether this is still in operation I have no idea, having had little or nothing to do with babies since. But the permanent lack of sleep causes extreme irritability and frustration mounting almost to a manic state. It is easy to understand how some women become frantic and physically abuse their babies. It is horrendous, of course, but one can understand how it happens. The incessant crying and wailing of an ever-demanding baby is bad enough on its own, but if there are other children to cope with as well then it must be almost intolerable.

I suppose some women must have a stronger maternal instinct then others. I am definitely one of the others. I was a very firm mother, and my insistence on discipline would always astonish visiting friends and acquaintances. At six o'clock I would simply say to my son, 'Time for bed', and he would go upstairs without a murmur. Maybe it was the thought of the inevitable bedtime story which prompted such instantaneous obedience – but it certainly produced a good effect on the assembled company, who would sit there flabbergasted!

Some women are attracted to powerful men. Not me: I need to be the powerful one. I am quite certain that my son does not fear me and has never feared me. I think he has a healthy respect for my temper. He's got quite a temper himself. He always says that he used to be frightened of me, but as he now regards me with a sort of amused contempt I find this hard to believe. We certainly get on very well. There was a time during his adolescence – always an extremely painful process – when things were not so good, but we've come through that and now I am in the happy position of being able to work with him too. I like to work with people whom I know very well, whom I am very close to or very fond of. A kind of mental shorthand operates; one knows that they are on the same wavelength and one doesn't have to go into lengthy explanations, as they will probably understand immediately what one is going to say.

Because I am not a typical mother, I also get on very well with my son's girlfriends. Indeed I shared a house with one of them, Jenny Agutter; she became a great friend and I was extremely fond of her. I am the same size as his current girlfriend, and because I have a tendency to buy clothes that are too young for me she inherits quite a few of the snazzier garments. I must admit she looks much better in them than I do!

Readers would be justified in feeling that I've had a rough ride with the male companions in my life. But Dickon is certainly one man with whom I've had no difficulty establishing a long-lasting relationship.

6

The Outer Woman – Clothes, Hair and Make-up

I spend my life dressing up, either for the stage or the camera, so I don't want to think about clothes in what I laughingly refer to as real life. I usually acquire stuff from any modern television drama in which I happen to be appearing. This obviates the need to go shopping. Shopping of any kind, but particularly for clothes, is to me tedious in the extreme. I occasionally pick up the odd garment that I take a fancy to when I am least expecting it, and certainly not when I am looking for anything. But this does not mean that I don't like to make a statement with what I wear. My taste in clothes in general is exotic. By that I mean out of the ordinary, unusual. I remember at the age of nineteen or twenty virtually stopping the traffic in the Aldwych because I was garbed in sludge green doublet and hose and medieval boots. On top of this I was wearing a chestnut-coloured cloak which was slung over one shoulder and fastened with a large copper brooch. As I had waist-length red hair at the time, and as London was still in the throes of being ultra-conservative, sartorially speaking, my outfit attracted a great deal of comment.

I may be uninterested in buying clothes, but I am very handy with a needle and thread and I'm a great fiddler with garments I already possess. The life of one's wardrobe can be extended quite considerably by dyeing clothes. But I never use the dyes just as they come, preferring to make really unusual mixtures by blending, say, very dark green with smoky grey to achieve a sort of jungle green, army fatigue look. Prune is another good colour, achieved by mixing purple with grey and brown. One has to experiment a little first by mixing colours in a jam jar with hot water and dropping a little piece of white fabric into the mixture to see what colour it is going to cme out. I recommend dyeing in the washing machnine – it is the only way to make the garments come out evenly coloured. It is important to wet the garments thoroughly before putting them in the machine. At the end, wipe out the machine with bleach and put an old tea towel or something of that nature through the hottest washing programme to pick up any left-over dye. When wearing your dye-it-yourself garments the trick is to wear one dyed garment with either something new and white, or certainly something new – never two dyed garments together.

Things in shops always seem to be a different colour when you get them home. I recently bought a linen suit under the impression that it was brown, but it turned out to be dull red – not a colour that suits me. I immediately went out and bought a packet of dark brown dye, flung the thing into the machine, and the result was a suit of the most wonderful burnt umber – a colour that has become immensely fashionable.

Tee-shirts and/or working clothes can have a wonderful new lease of life when dyed a really zingy colour or alternatively a really off-beat sombre shade. Come to think of it I seldom buy anything that I don't alter in some way or another the moment I get it home. I am quite ruthless. I yank shoulder pads out if I don't like them, or alternatively insert them if I am not happy with the cut of the shoulder. I invariably shorten the skirts of almost every garment I buy. I wear my skirts very short, and have done ever since 1963 I suppose. I have never followed fashion, but have for the last two decades always found my own style and stuck to it in a rather boring manner. I amputate sleeves as well, or wear those rather nifty little men's elasticated wire bands to push a sleeve up. I don't think I have ever been seen with a sleeve below my elbow – perhaps just below, but certainly not to my wrist. I turn coats and jackets into jerkins when I am bored with them by ripping out their sleeves and cutting them off to thigh level.

I dye shoes as well as clothes, or paint them to match various outfits; if I can't get the exact colour I want in the right size and style of shoe, I simply buy the shoe in any shade and paint it the required colour. One of my greatest delights is matching my evening shoes to my evening dresses. And I spend hours mixing dyes to get exactly the right shade, usually a very subtle colour to dye my satin court shoes which are bought specially for the purpose, originally a pristine white.

I remake garments inside out to give them a different look, usually a faded version of their original selves. I am very into faded. On the whole I prefer muted, faded, subtle colours and seldom wear bright hues. I have one brief outbreak of colour each summer, particularly when I go abroad, when I suddenly burst into bright lime, lurid tangerine and amazing turquoise, but this does not last very long. I find it a bit demanding, I soon get tired of it all and I gradually slip back into my sludge grey, green and blues. I am very fond of white – I like the neutrality. I

109

find I can live up to it; in other words I provide the colour myself with my face, skin and hair.

I dress up, of course, for the evening (probably with a pair of those dyed-to-match shoes underneath) if I am going out to the theatre to be a member of the audience for a change. I have many functions to attend and, as I have two production companies of my own, many business meetings as well. I have a couple of good suits for this purpose and numerous other rather glamorous outfits which get a public airing whenever I have to make a personal appearance.

Finding suitable clothes for these occasions is an eternal headache. I spent my last £300 on buying an outfit in which to meet the casting director of *Dynasty*. What would I have done if I had not got the job? But that is the sort of chance I love to take in life, and almost always pays off. As for the personal appearances, which of course includes chat shows on TV, and even when one is being interviewed on radio, one has to look splendid, as photographs are invariably taken and one doesn't like to disappoint the interviewer. Also one has some sort of reputation to keep up, I think.

When one is doing a programme like *Dynasty* or *Howard's Way*, one usually finds the costume department more than willing to help out in this area. It is, after all, in their interests that their artists look good. Some of the amazing creations that I was loaned from the stockroom at Warner Bros in Hollywood defy description. I remember in particular one garment which was made of skin-tight, skin-coloured gauze, slashed up to the knee and down to the navel and covered entirely with gold bugle beads – a sort of Marlene Dietrich creation. I wore it for a photographic session and was then lent it again for a televised promotion for *Dynasty*. Everything was fine to start with; a lot of the cast were assembled in the Carrington mansion, in the hall at the bottom of the staircase, and then to my horror I saw Linda Evans coming down the stairs in an identical number except that

110

she was covered in silver bugle beads. It was obviously a popular Hollywood garment for such occasions and had been much favoured by the wardrobe department over the years!

Howard's Way of course, is a rather different kettle of fish. It aims, I think, to occupy a sort of British *Dynasty* spot, and there is indeed a great deal of emphasis put on the sartorial aspect of the show – but in a somewhat less obvious vein, thiank God. The costume department is very obliging and seems keen to have me looking good when appearing on, say, the *Wogan* show or something of that ilk.

For rehearsals I invariably wear dance practice gear. I find this very comfortable and generally liberating, in as much as that it allows total freedom of movement. For everyday life, when not actually working, I live in jeans and tee-shirts or sweat-shirts and Reeboks. I only ever wear tights when I have to wear a skirt.

I believe one should dress to please oneself, and for me that means being comfortable and best fitted to accommodate my extremely-full life. I often take changes of clothes with me on my various trips so that I don't, for example, have to rehearse in the same clothes which I have used for a more glamorous occasion. My schedule is invariably so heavy that I normally have to do at least two things on the same day, usually three or four plus a show in the evening. Because I am not really interested in clothes I am often inappropriately dressed, and my better-attired girlfriends despair of me!

My interest in my professional clothes, on the other hand, knows no bounds. I am meticulous about the attention to detail in a period costume. This is all part of my love of history and, of course, my total dedication to work.

My hair, like my disinterest in clothes, has been a source of irritation to my friends for years. You see, I won't cut it. It sort of cuts itself now and again, because it gets so fed up with hanging around that it breaks off as a sort of protest. Occasionally as a great favour I allow some trusted make-up artist to snip the tiniest bit off the ends. But I watch them like a hawk. I am a bit like Samson really – I know that if I lost my hair I would be defeated.

I once had a ghastly experience. I went to a hairdresser with lovely long locks. I only went to have some highlights put in, but they said that it was all burning and disintegrating and they cut off about eight inches. I was suicidal for weeks. The result is that, no matter how people may loathe it and try to persuade me to the contrary, my hair is now and will always be, for ever and ever amen, *long*. Either short long, medium long or very long. At the moment it is medium long, but I am persevering and soon it will be very long again. I know it is extremely unsuitable for my years, and that's another thing I don't care about!

I suppose that because I am a Leo I am really trying to cultivate a kind of lion's mane. This is an ongoing struggle between my hair and myself, because my hair's one desire in life is to be left alone to lie down smoothly and quietly and go to sleep. But that is not for me. I grab it, I colour it red, gold, brown, I backcomb it, I tease it, I lacquer it, I persuade it, I curl it, I Carmen it, I perm it. It has an unendurable life with me, but I win most of the time. I wash my hair about twice a week and condition it lavishly – this is by way of apology for the browbeating it has received until then. Henna is my latest passion. I have found that it seems to condition and thicken the hair and so I subject my mane to this extraordinary treatment. It's rather like putting several tons of mud on your head, but it works.

There are only two people whom I'm happy to let loose on my hair – though not, of course, with scissors in their hands. One is my make-up artist and hairdresser on *Howard's Way*, Paul Gooch, and the other is a lady called Janice. She lives in a most delightful little house with a very accommodating husband and baby and a completely mad dog called Scooby Doo. I trust her with my eccentric locks for the simple reason that she has a head of the most glorious hair herself. She also does exactly what I want. My visits to her are a joy. I sit in her kitchen and we gossip away happily while she transforms my recalcitrant straight barnet into a wild cornucopia of tumbling curls.

Men often claim that they prefer women without make-up. They love the natural, fresh look, they say. I have fallen for this line several times in my life, with the result that I have been persuaded actually to venture into public and foist the real me on to the unsuspecting citizen. Feeling thoroughly naked and uncomfortable in a crowded bar or restaurant somewhere, I then become aware that my partner is spending the entire evening gazing in completely undisguised, blatant admiration, not to say adoration, at a female across the room who has enough make-up on to sink a battleship. I have learnt my lesson.

There are times when I do appear completely unmade up and enjoy it very much, but on the whole I feel better with it. I usually put on the most make-up to go to bed – it gives me confidence. I enjoy putting on make-up: it's rather like painting a picture. I paint the picture of the person I would really like to be, a person who is infinitely better-looking than the real me. I always use products that don't involve testing on animals, so I buy mainly from the Body Shop or health food stores.

It's mainly the eyes, of course. I developed my technique in applying eye make-up by studying the Italians. They were, if you remember, great artists themselves, especially at the time of the Renaissance. My role models, however, were Sophia Loren, Elsa Martinelli, Virna Lisi and a Teutonic lady, Ursula Andress. My eye make-up has always been heavy, dramatic and with a decided tendency towards the slantingly exotic. That is because my eyes are deep-set and narrow. I think it is important to emphasise one's best features to make the most of them, so I make the most of my cheekbones and my eyes and my high forehead. My eyebrows lead a life entirely of their own devising – they are so recalcitrant and wayward that I am forced to glue them into shape. I literally apply tiny specks of eyelash glue and then brush the hairs straight up after the manner of the glorious Sophia.

I outline my eyes firmly and with great determination in the face of a lot of opposition from producers, directors, lighting men, camera men, relatives, dubious girlfriends and advice from magazines. I draw the top line very close to the eyelashes and continue it beyond the end of the eye, slanting upwards as though I were about to essay the role of Ariel in *The Tempest* (1). I then do the same with the bottom line, making it join the top line and slanting it right up (2).

I then take very fine, widely spaced false eyelashes and glue them as close to my own eyelashes as possible following this slanting line (3). When they are firmly in place and have dried, I then glue my own eyelashes to the false eyelashes (4). This has the effect of opening up the eye at the side and gives the appearance of a startled nymph. As I have always harboured the secret yearning to be such a creature, this has precisely the results I desire. Because I have no socket and my lids are very deep-set, I pencil in where the socket should be with a very dark brown pencil, again in a forthright manner brooking no argument from anyone, and that line also goes to meet its fellows (5). I then smudge it around a bit (6).

This look has not really been in fashion since about 1972. But that does not deter me – it's a look that suits me, and I am sticking with it.

Likewise my mouth. Pale lipstick was all the rage around 1968 for about one year, but so far as I am concerned it's here for ever. I outline my lips in a sort of ambery brown pencil, to the horror of all and sundry. I then also outline the inner part of the upper lip in the same pencil. Finally I fill in the whole mouth with the palest beigy-peachy-toffeeish sort of colour that I can lay my hands on. Needless to say, the moment I have found a colour that is absolutely right for me, and is usually called something like Nude Tango or Bolero Buff, they stop making it. But

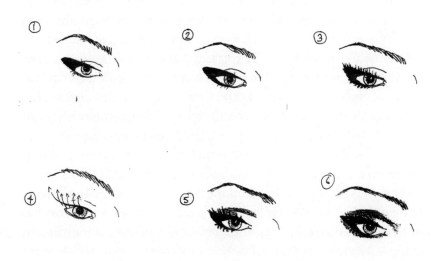

undaunted I scour the make-up counters until I find a substitute. I have tried darker lipsticks, but all to no avail. I look like a whore. Of course on the stage this is an entirely different matter, but here I am referring to that extraordinary sequence of events known as everyday life.

I always carefully paint out with concealer any lines or bags or other unwanted intrusions. I put some of the same concealer across the tops of my cheekbones to accentuate them, and I use a bronzed blusher under my cheekbones and at my temples. I seldom wear make-up base on the rest of my face. If I don't have any natural freckles (and I usually do) I paint them on, particularly on my nose. That too is a fashion left over from 1968, and I don't care.

When I go out for a big occasion in public, or a party, I really go to town on the make-up – I do the full Hollywood glamour bit. You would be amazed at the amount of make-up it is possible to get on to my face. I have quite a large face, so there is plenty of scope. I use every trick known to woman, from lip gloss and gleamer to eyebrow and eye highlighter, to blusher on the temples and under the chin, to three coats of mascara with powdering in between each application to make it thicker.

Where TV make-up is concerned, I always do my own. I am totally proprietorial about it. Paul Gooch from *Howard's Way*, for instance, who is so good at doing my hair, watches and makes helpful comments every now and again, but I completely ignore them. I have been making up this tired old face for many years now and will continue to do so until I drop – I have grown accustomed to my face and know exactly how to beat it into submission.

And how do I get all that make-up off again? For me there's one golden rule – I never put soap on my face, ever. I bathe it in hot water in the mornings and I give it a little gentle covering of some sort of moisturiser. I remove my make-up with oil and I exfoliate the facial skin about once every two weeks. I also use a body scrub at about the same intervals. It makes the skin wonderfully smooth and I am sure is very good for it.

I have not yet had a face lift, but I have not entirely ruled out the possibility. Some people might call it vanity, of course, but I would look upon it as an extension to my working life; obviously the longer I can remain looking younger, the better my chances of working. However, I have to say I am apprehensive and am putting it off for the moment. The women I have seen who have had face lifts look quite wonderful – it's not that they look younger, it's simply that they look better. I don't think there is anything wrong or self-indulgent about wanting to improve one's looks. One only gets one shot at it, after all, and we'll be dead a long time, so why not make the most of it while we're here? And if improving one's looks also improves the quality of one's life, I think there's a great deal to be said for it.

I know it is considered inadvisable nowadays, but I do frequent the sun bed. I have a naturally very fair skin, due to my

Celtic origins, and I find that few sessions on the sun bed before venturing into very hot sun will build up my resistance to burning. Apart from anything else I prefer to be brown, or at least beige. I do, however, try not to expose my face too much, because I think that over-exposure to the sun's rays, whether natural or unnatural, can result in premature ageing of the skin. But in general I look better when I am tanned, I feel better when I am tanned, and so I go for it.

I am not too good about nails. I lead an extremely active life, which involves things like bricklaying, demolition work, typing, playing the piano, sewing, hitting fellow actors, putting up and taking down scenery, and moving things. I am always moving things, particularly furniture. I long ago realised that I had missed my vocation in life: I was born to be a removal man. I have even moved a baby grand piano on my own. Occasionally I do a bit of gardening. I like going for long walks and hacking my way through brambles and undergrowth. You may deduce from all this that my nails really don't stand a chance. Not for me the elegant red talons so favoured by traditional glamour girls – they would impede my facility in all these activities. So I go around with short, practical, naturally coloured, ordinary nails. I loathe nail polish except on my toenails.

I visit the beauty parlour about twice a year, once at Christmas and once near my birthday. This is for a manicure and pedicure. It's my way of indulging myself. I visit the hairdresser under duress and extreme pressure only about once every five years and only if frog-marched there and back. My hair of course gets done for me when I am working either in television or in movies and when I am appearing on stage I wear wigs and hair-pieces. However, when featuring in that elusive half world known as real life, I attend to my toilet myself invariably. Beauty parlours and hairdressing salons somehow seem to manage without my patronage, so I can find no good reason to give them my custom. I'm too independent, and I just like doing things my way.

7

The Inner Woman: Diet and Exercise

Most of my life I have been a shy and insecure person. This statement may seem ludicrous, but I can assure you it is true. I camouflage this deep-rooted inferiority complex quite successfully, I think. There is doubtless some Freudian explanation for it all and I dare say a few visits to the psychiatrist would reveal all. However, I have neither the time nor the money to indulge myself thus. Suffice it to say that I have had to overcome these feelings over the years. I am not alone in this – a lot of actors feel this way. Indeed the reason why many of them become actors is that they don't like themselves very much and prefer to play other people. It is certainly so in my case.

My conversion to vegetarianism was an early attempt to make myself interesting. It is only in subsequent years that I have become aware of the ecological, sociological and moral implications. When I was in my late teens, everybody that I knew smoked. So as to appear different and therefore supposedly interesting, I decided I would not smoke. I never have and never will. After the privation of the war, when I was in my teens, people suddenly became health-conscious again and allowed themselves the luxury of choosing what they wished to eat. It was then that health food shops started to emerge. As I had hardly any money at the time, I decided it would be better to eat little but very healthily. This of course made me different, not to say, eccentric. In those days, one was described as a crank if one went in for this sort of behaviour.

By the time we had reached the sixties with their flower power, hippies, CND and make-love-not-war ethic, I was already well into the other craze of the time, which was vegetarianism. People became concerned not only about the plight of the starving millions in Africa, but also about the countless animals suffering in laboratories. It has taken a further twenty years for people to become aware of the wholesale manner in which we are destroying our planet, but thank God we are at last realising just what we are doing to ourselves. Sociologically and ecologically, it is going to become imperative that we grow more crops for people to eat and reduce the numbers of livestock who at present are devouring those crops so uneconomically. Crops fed directly to human beings go a lot further than the same crops fed to animals whose meat is then eaten by people. This means that meat will become a luxury item, only available to the very rich. On a moral level, I believe that until we cease our oppression of the animals who are unable to defend themselves we have very little chance of being humane to each other. We are all fellow creatures on this planet, and must somehow learn to co-exist if we and the planet are to survive.

On a more selfish note, vegetarianism has another advantage

120

– it helps one to stay slim. Anyone who imagines that there is an easy way to diet is kidding themselves. There is only one surefire diet and that is a permanent one – in other words 'diet', not 'a diet'. It requires willpower, determination, nerves of steel and above all vanity. And it means re-educating your approach to food.

Food should be regarded in the same way as cleaning one's teeth – as a necessary part of life rather than a pleasure to be indulged in. Ever since we were first exposed to the horrors of starvation and malnutrition in the Third World in the early sixties I have ceased to be interested in food. I was so consumed with guilt at my good fortune in being able to eat what I wanted that I lost all interest in eating. By this I do not mean that I became anorexic, it was simply that food ceaased to be enjoyable to me. I now eat only when it is absolutely necessary – in other words, only when I am hungry. Comfort, pleasure or social reasons do not justify eating.

The easiest way to put on weight is to eat after six o'clock; the second easiest is to eat breakfast. This goes against all the advice given by dieticians and doctors, but it has proved to be so in my experience. It is only necessary to eat one and a half meals a day, or better still two half meals a day: a small amount at lunchtime and a small amount at, say, five o'clock. This way you use up the food you've eaten and your body has no difficulty in digesting it.

There is another way of losing weight very quickly which I have found to be efficacious, and that is to go on a fast. Fasting is very good: one can obtain bags of energy this way, and the results around the hip area are extremely satisfying. Of course one of the easiest methods of fasting is to be involved in an unhappy love affair: the flesh simply drops off, possibly through misery. Even to be involved in a happy love affair seems to be beneficial in this department, so I suppose even if love affairs don't have much else to recommend them, at least they are a good way of maintaining the perfect figure – whatever that may be.

GAME PLAN

I firmly believe that we all eat too much. I have been a vegetarian for practically the whole of my adult life and, contrary to popular belief about such people, I am not grey-looking or pasty-faced or sunken-eyed or particularly scraggy. On the contrary, I think I look quite healthy. People tell me it is quite impossible to live without eating meat. They seem to be unaware of the fact that I am living proof that it is possible. I no longer even eat fish, and have not done so for about fifteen years. I have one vice and it is a terrible one – I drink China tea with brown sugar! But I think I'm allowed one. It is my main pleasure in life – gastronomically that is. It is a source of great comfort to me, and I am fully aware that it is a drug and that I am hooked for life. Coffee holds no such charms for me. I can take it or leave it, but not tea. I must have tea. I require tea at least twice a day.

I am a great believer in the whole food diet; by that I mean a high fibre diet. I exist mainly on avocado pears, stone-ground brown bread, bean curd, salad, fruit, yoghurt and vegetables. Bean curd or tofu, particularly the smoked variety, makes a wonderful meal especially when chopped up with apple, watercress, raw mushrooms or whatever raw vegetable you can find, and sprinkled with lemon juice. It is also very good fried with garlic, though I am not a great advocate of fried foods – that is only for very special occasions.

My greatest delight is the avocado. I am convinced it is because I spent the first two years of my life in the West Indies that I have a passion for avocados and pineapple juice and bananas and coconut milk. Diced avocados, with sliced up oranges and watercress or any form of a salad leaf, is one of the most refreshing and nourishing meals I know.

The two meals I have described above, bean curd salad and avocado salad, are my staple diet. I live on them day in, day out. I alternate them, add to or subtract from them, and this, plus the odd bit of stone-ground bread, the odd banana, some of the dishes for which recipes are given below, and my precious cups of tea is what I live on. I think I am living proof that it is a healthy diet. I do believe that you are what you eat – so OK, I am as mad as a hatter, but I *am* very fit!

Dutch House Salad

Peel, stone and slice two avocados. Peel two oranges and slice in rounds. Toss some rocket, lamb's lettuce or endive in French dressing. Add the avocados and orange slices, top with chopped fresh mint and serve immediately.

Prickly Green Salad

Peel and grate one raw beetroot. Peel and chop one cooking apple. Skin and finely chop one small onion. Mix all together and add a handful of sultanas. Toss in fresh lemon juice and olive oil and serve.

Salade Nathalie

Chop 1lb (450g) of cooked spinach. Peel and chop one small onion. Peel and chop one cooking apple. Blanch and peel 1 lb (450g) of tomatoes and chop. Mix all these ingredients together and scatter over the salad broken pieces of Gorgonzola or other blue cheese. This one looks revolting but tastes delicious.

Cauliflower Soup

Gently cook two small cloves of garlic in a knob of vegetable margarine in a frying pan. Add a small peeled, chopped onion. Add half a cauliflower, cut into florets. Leave to tenderise for a few minutes. Make up a pint (600ml) of vegetable stock and milk, mixed. Add to the cauliflower and stir in well. Cover and leave to simmer gently for 15 minutes. Remove from the heat and liquidise. Return to the heat and add black pepper and sea salt to taste. Serve sprinkled liberally with cayenne.

Audley Soup
Gently cook a clove of garlic in a knob of vegetable margarine in a saucepan. Simmer 8oz (250g) of frozen peas with a sprig of fresh mint. Add half a lettuce, chopped, and blanch in the same water. Remove from the heat and liquidise. Add half a cup of single cream and return to the heat, but do not boil. Remove from the heat and garnish with chopped fresh mint. This soup is good either hot or chilled in summer.

Summer Treat
Mix together 8oz (250g) curd cheese, 2 large (500g) cartons of natural yoghurt, 6 tablespoons of runny honey and 4oz (125g) of mixed hazelnuts and walnuts, ground. Leave to set in a bowl in the fridge overnight. Lightly cook in some brown sugar 1lb (500g) of mixed blackberries, redcurrants and blackcurrants. Do not overcook. Serve the cooked fruit hot on top of the cold ice cream.

Mincemeat
Chop two large cooking apples (do not peel) and 4oz (125g) walnuts. Add the zest of two oranges and two lemons, 8oz (250g) of sultanas and 8oz (250g) of currants. Cook this mixture in dark brown sugar and honey to taste for 20 minutes. Then add some grated nutmeg, a teaspoon of ground ginger, a teaspoon of ground cinnamon (or cinnamon stick) and a few cloves and simmer for a further 20 minutes. Remove any whole spices used and put in clean, sterilised jam jars.

I also consume vast quantities of Aqua Libra. I drink it like water and instead of water, and as its name means free water, that's quite appropriate. It is quite simply wonderful. If this sounds like an advertisement, which I suppose it is, then I shall expect several cases of the stuff by way of recompense from the manufacturers.

My life becomes complicated when I am working, because it is often very difficult to find any of the foods I eat on a canteen or restaurant menu. So I am obliged either to bring my own food with me to work, or to make do with some yoghurt or fruit or the odd bit of vegetable if I am feeling adventurous – except they are usually overcooked and highly unpleasant. I sometimes just have Ryvita and cheese and an apple at lunchtime, which I find works quite well for me.

People are always very concerned about my eating habits. I am inclined to eat standing up, and if I do join them at table they always remark on the paucity of my diet. It upsets me that I insist on indulging in such socially unacceptable behaviour but I think that although people always do comment they are getting used to me now.

I am not perhaps the world's best hostess when it comes to entertaining people by offering them food. I dare say that if one enjoys shopping around for the various ingredients, and the preparation and the cooking, it could all be quite rewarding. But I fear that my selfishness is about to rear its ugly head again. I really don't enjoy cooking – I am simply not interested in it. I find a sort of quiet satisfaction in rustling up something for people who eat when they visit me – but it has to be prepared and consumed at break-neck speed, the plates are whipped away from the unsuspecting visitor with what can only be described as sleight of hand, and washed up while they are still swallowing their last mouthful.

On the rare occasions when I do entertain, or at any rate prepare a meal for someone, I have noticed with some perplexity

125

the reluctance of men in particular to tuck in. It is one of life's great mysteries. The moment that the food is on the table, cooked to perfection and piping hot, every male member of the household completely disappears from sight. They start opening bottles of wine, going to the loo, 'just popping out for a minute', or any number of other paltry excuses. Anything to delay the moment when they actually sit down to eat, even though they have been demanding in rather petulant tones for at least twenty minutes when lunch was going to be ready. One can only assume that they are endorsing Jane Austen's maxim – something to do with the pleasure of realization seldom exceeding the pleasure of anticipation. Whatever the reason, it's bloody infuriating, and in my experience it's a common male trait!

Along with eating too much, I believe we all sleep too much. The reason we need to sleep a lot is because we have eaten too much, and the body has to have time to digest what it has eaten. In the process it gets exhausted and then has to sleep it off. If we ate less we would need to sleep less, and then we would have all those extra hours in which to enjoy life; and if we were slim and fit and healthy then life would indeed be enjoyable.

A healthy body encourages a healthy mind. The early hours of the morning are some of the most valuable, in my opinion; even if one only spends them collecting one's thoughts contemplating, meditating, taking stock, they are times well spent. They can also be spent exercising. It is only necessary to exercise for twenty minutes or half an hour in the morning and the same at night to maintain a trim figure. It doesn't have to be rigorous or demanding – it is simply a matter of limbering up, of keeping thinks in working order by merely stretching and toning the muscles.

The parts of a woman's body that seem most vulnerable to deterioration are the hips, stomach and thighs. These are the parts that are concerned with child-bearing, and as we have been victims of our biological situation for so long it is a truly wonderful feeling to overcome the limitations imposed on us by nature. I think the contraceptive pill has been instrumental in women's liberation, and hormone replacement therapy is pushing away other barriers. But more of that anon.

I think it is a good idea when exercising to wear leg-warmers. I wear really long ones that keep my ankles and knees warm, and in particular my calf muscles. It is very important to keep your leg muscles warm while you are exercising them; if not you may get cramp or, even worse, damage your muscles.

1

REACH   DROP   PUSH UP   DOWN

The first exercise I do is to stand with my feet apart and stretch my arms up to the ceiling. Then, bending at the knees, I pull my arms down until they touch the floor with the palms turned inwards, facing each other. Then I pull my legs straight and come up (1). I do this about ten times.

Still standing with my legs apart, I bring my arms up to shoulder level outstretched and swing several times to the left, so that I'm swinging around to face the wall behind me (2). I repeat this action about ten times one side and then reverse and do ten times the other way.

2

I then stretch one arm above my head and push over to one side ten times, and then alternate and do the other arm and push, bending over to the other side about ten times (3). I then go back to the previous exercise and then right back to the first exercise.

3

THE INNER WOMAN: DIET AND EXERCISE

It is important after each exercise to shake out your limbs and your whole body so that the muscles don't tense up with the effort.

I then lie on the floor on my back, put my hands behind my head and raise my legs slowly from the floor until they are stretched right above me at right-angles to my body. Then very slowly I lower them again until they almost reach the floor, but I don't let them touch it. I keep them very straight and raise them again until they are at right-angles, and lower them again (4). I do this twice, then after they have been lowered I bend them at the knees and pull them into the body. I don't at any time use my hands to help me. I repeat this exercise at least ten times.

4

LIFT   HOLD

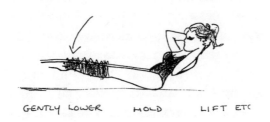

GENTLY LOWER   HOLD   LIFT ETC

It is very important after this one, to prevent the muscles clenching, that you should stretch out your body completely with your arms above your head and stretch your arms as far as you can to the right-hand side, bending the knees and stretching the lower half of the torso and the legs to the left side (5). Then swap over so that the muscles around the abdomen are stretched, so the arms stretch to the left-hand side while the knees are pulling the body to the right-hand side. Repeat this about five times, then relax.

5

Still lying flat on my back, I now draw my knees up so that they are bent but with the feet still on the floor. Keeping my hands behind my head, and indeed holding the back of my head by my neck, I then make my stomach pull the top half of my body up and back, lifting the top half of my body. But the arms must not help – it is the stomach muscles that must do the work. Up and down, up and down about twenty times without the head resting on the floor, and then relax; and then another twenty times, and then relax (6). Then repeat the abdomen-stretching exercise.

6

USING STOMACH
MUSCLES ONLY.

I then remain on the floor but turn on my side with my legs
stretched out and supporting myself on one elbow. I lift one leg
straight up and down about ten times, keeping the leg extended
and trying not to let it rest but making it work up and down at
least ten times (7). I then turn over and do it with the other leg.
This is very good for what I think are called love handles – the
little pads of flesh around the hip area. I repeat the exercise with
the other side and then go back again to the first side, so that I've
given them each a good going over.

7

A   B

8

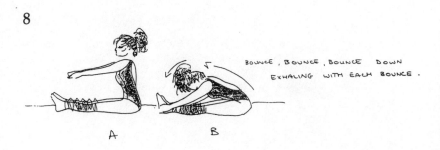

BOUNCE, BOUNCE, BOUNCE DOWN
EXHALING WITH EACH BOUNCE.

A   B

I then sit up on the floor with my legs stretched out straight in front of me and bend forward, trying to put my head on my knees and grasping my upturned toes. I then leave go and go slowly back until I am extended on my back. Then up again, head on knees, touching toes, back again, extended on floor, up again, head on knees, touching toes etc etc and so on (8). Again about twenty times. After this exercise I shake my legs out to relax the muscles.

The next exercise I do standing up with my legs apart. I drop to one side and clasp my right ankle with both my hands, putting my head on my right knee and up; then I move to the left side and do the same again, keeping the legs straight as before (9). I do this about ten times each side. At the end of that exercise I shake out both legs to relax them.

I then crouch on my haunches with my feet absolutely together. I clutch my ankles from the back with my hands and then, keeping my head down, I gradually pull up until the legs are straight, trying to keep my head on my knees all the while (10).

9

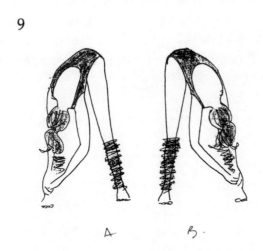

A   B.

10

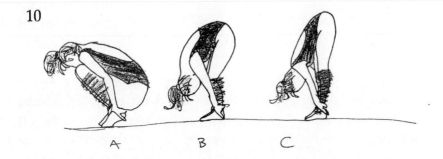

A   B   C

I then extend one leg behind me whilst bending the front one and put my hands on the floor, in the manner of a sprinter waiting for the starting gun. Keeping my hands on the floor I straighten the front leg (11). I do this ten times. Then I change over legs, extend the other leg behind me, bend the front one and, keeping my hands on the floor, straighten the front leg. Again I shake my legs after this exercise.

11

STRAIGHTEN FRONT LEG + PUSH BOTTOM UP

Next, I lie down on the floor again on my side, supporting myself on one elbow. I bend the uppermost leg in towards me, clutch my instep and pull the leg up straight (12). I repeat this ten times. I then turn over and do the other leg. Again I shake out my legs after the exercise.

12

By now all the muscles are aching wonderfully, so I sit up and sort of walk on my bum. I draw my legs up and, supporting myself on my hands, I work my way for about ten paces forward and ten paces back but sitting on my bum (13). This is very good for getting rid of any cellulite that might be causing problems. You may have noticed that most of my exercises are to do with the stomach, hips and leg area. These are the parts I am most concerned with and, particularly if one has a sedentary occupation, they are the areas which receive the least attention and get the least amount of exercise.

13

8

Home-making O'Mara Style

As a child I think I spent every year of my life moving from place to place. We always moved at least once a year, sometimes more frequently, and we certainly never spent more than one year in any one place. I spent a lot of my time at boarding school or away from home for one reason or another, and I think this has given me a rather peripatetic approach to life. I am a nomad. Rootless, really. I can't seem to settle. As an adult I move from place to place – restlessly seeking something permanent, I suppose. However, with every place that I move to I always manage to make a home, however temporarily. I move into a place and within a very short space of time I have completely transformed it. I knock down walls, I remove doors and windows. I demolish fireplaces, I remodel the entire building until it suits me.

I hasten to add that I am not a vandal. On the contrary I am a restorer, a protector, a preserver. My mission in life is to restore old houses to their former glory, something I have done on many occasions. I work tirelessly but almost effortlessly, day and night, beavering away until I have effected the transformation. Friends who have been planning minor cosmetic alterations to their abodes for years marvel in disbelief at the total transmogrification of my dwelling places. They stand agape as they see the havoc I have wrought, and then gaze in awe and wonder at the phoenix that rises from the ashes in what is inevitably and invariably a very short time indeed.

I have a passion for green which I would go so far as to call an obsession. Not just any old green, you understand, but a green that is redolent of dark forests and the Dark Ages. It has to conjure up a mysterious, primeval, timeless wood, and if I am surrounded by this colour I am happy – for a while. Over the years I have tried different colours, but they have not worked and I have not been happy. I can thoroughly recommend green: it is one of nature's own colours and therefore very easy to live with. For obvious reasons it goes very well with almost any wood. Grey is also very good and understanding. It makes a pleasant neutral background, but a greenish grey is best of all.

This preoccupation has driven most of my cohabitors quietly mad; for some reason they seem to like colours like white, cream, beige, or light, bright, optimistic colours like orange and yellow, even pink and blue. I have tried very hard to come to terms with this rainbow existence, but to no avail. I persevere for a while, and then one day in a frantic fit of frenzy I grab a paintbrush, everything is returned to a strange, wonderful, smoky Celtic twilight, and life is bearable again.

I think it is very pleasant to have white or cream furniture and white or cream carpets. Totally impractical, but very useful. This

way you can change the colours of the walls as often as you like –
unless of course, like me, you are obsessed with one particular
colour. But it does mean that you can alter your colour scheme as
your mood takes you merely by chucking different-coloured
cushions around or, as in my case, painting a huge living room
in a space of about two hours. I work very quickly, as all my
friends will witness.

In my house (perhaps I should say in my houses plural
because I move so frequently) there is a lot of evidence of me and
my career around. I dare say that some people might find this a
touch vain – in fact the amount of evidence of my theatrical
endeavours is possibly verging on megalomania – but I find it
reassuring. These are the only sort of memorabilia that I allow
myself. I have kept no personal memories of any past associa-
tions. The only photographs I have are of plays or movies on
which I have worked. I have only one or two photographs of
myself with my son; there are no baby photographs of either him
or me, and I have no photographs of my family or indeed of my
friends. This may seem strange, but the past to me is something
that happened and I have no wish to remember it. The present
and the future are what is important.

It comes as a surprise to most people that I am in any way
domesticated. But certain aspects of it I enjoy. I love painting
and decorating, I like making curtains, upholstering furniture,
putting up shelves, demolishing walls. I have even in my time
done some bricklaying and indeed plastering – not entirely
successfully, but I have had a go. I once built a garden wall with a
great deal of success. I am very good at moving rubble. One of
the greatest joys of my life is visiting rubbish tips, and I love
chucking things out: it is wonderfully therapeutic.

Although I hate cooking I will do it from time to time, in fact I
am really quite a good cook. I can make bread and I can make
jam, so long as I don't have to do it on a regular basis, I can cope.

I enjoy housework. I like things to be clean and tidy and

ordered – in my home, that is. Anyone who has seen my dressing room at a theatre will know that this sense of tidiness does not include my theatrical activities! I give extremely clean performances – by which I mean performances that are clear and economic – but I fear that my dressing table is a pigsty. There is no other word for it. I have never been able to fathom why. I suppose a psychologist would say that my home, which is always tidy and clean and pristine, is more important to me than my career. And they might well be right. I am notoriously unsuccessful in my attempts to create home life and have been really quite remarkably successful in my career. As always, I imagine it's simply a matter of survival.

My idea of a perfect house is one in which one can relax comfortably and look at beautiful objects; therefore I like to have modern/classic comfortable furniture, but I like to look at beautiful antiques and pictures. And, as I've said earlier, antique hunting is one of my passions. I like mirrors, too. They add space and dimension, give a different view of things, reflect light and can make a small room seem twice as big. I like open fires or pretend open fires, which give warmth and create a focus for the room. I dislike television sets; they are conversation stoppers and can distract dreadfully. I either put them in separate rooms or in the bedroom as television is wonderfully soporific.

I try to be eclectic. I love the idea of a modern painting above a very old piece of furniture. I always try to arrange it so that any modern plain armchair that I have in a room is flanked on either side by antique furniture. They make a wonderful foil for each other and set each other off perfectly.

I am not terribly happy about cut flowers. I prefer to see them growing in their natural habitat. But I do like greenhouse plants and dried flowers. I prefer to put dried flower in unusual places, such as on the tops of cupboards and ornate mirrors. I always go for the dramatic effect in my various houses. Maybe one day I will have a permanent home. It had better be soon – I am running out of time. But for the moment, these temporary abodes are always furnished with love and care, a great deal of attention to detail, and, I like to think, a certain amount of artistic flair. They are also usually quite dramatic in appeal.

It is possibly because I am a Leo that I go for the dramatic effect. I certainly go for the grand and the grandiose and the rich and opulent look. My bedroom is nearly always theatrical: not necessarily sexy or vampish, but I do rather go in for four-posters and drapes and a generally Jacobean look. Ideally a bed should be huge, for all sorts of reasons. I am quite happy if the bed occupies most of the the bedroom. Some people have this extraordinary idea that it is necessary for a bedroom to have places in which to keep clothes. I find one small cupboard sufficient, but then I am not interested in clothes and I suppose those who are would need more than that.

I hate cold bathrooms; they should be warm, welcoming places, always carpeted and preferably painted in warm colours, or better still wallpapered. Bathrooms should not be dismissed as functional places but should receive as much loving care and attention as the rest of the house. It is very restful, reassuring and relaxing to soak in a hot bath and gaze at a beautiful picture. My houses are always extremely warm, for I am a very cold person and require a great deal of warmth. My central heating bills are usually fairly high, but then I don't drink or smoke and I don't eat much, so I think I am entitled to that particular luxury in life.

There are several people in my life without whom my existence would be virtually untenable. Firstly, there is Christine, who virtually runs my life. It is difficult to describe her exact role: I suppose one could say that she is a sort of Girl Friday, although she would add 'and Saturday, Sunday, Monday, Tuesday, Wednesday, Thursday'. She organises me completely, and what I did before I met her I cannot imagine. Then there is Clive. As I have already mentioned, I spend a great deal of my time moving house. As with clothes and furniture, I am never satisfied with any house that I buy and drastic alteration has to be undertaken before I can make it my own. This is where Clive comes into his own. No architectural extravaganza of whatever proportions or preposterousness can daunt him. His favourite phrase is 'Anything is possible, Kate.' I take him at his word and together we have created a number of little gems for posterity to enjoy.

After Clive has wrought his miracles I arm myself with a paintbrush and a sewing machine. A great deal of money can be saved by making one's own curtains, and indeed recovering one's own furniture, making cushions, drapes and so on. In the old days when I was young and easy under the apple boughs, I used to make my own clothes, but as I think I have already mentioned, clothes no longer interest me, so I have stopped that particular activity. But the same rule applies, press after sewing anything or pinning anything or tacking anything, and measure frequently. Really dramatic effects can be achieved by making a pair of curtains in a fairly bold pattern (say a floral print) and then lining them with a small trellis design. These can hug the inside part of the window on a perfectly ordinary curtain fitting. Then you can put up a pole on the outside of the window and use a contrasting material, or an antique scarf or shawl, as a drape across the pole.

I'm not just an ideas person; I know all the practical tricks, too, that make all the difference to the finished result. I press seams and hems constantly to make them crisp and even. One cannot press too often. Nor can one measure too often – for some unknown reason material takes on a life of its own, especially with curtains. Hems drop and ride up at random. So it is best to measure to start with, pin the required length, press the hem, measure again, sew it, press again, and then hang the curtain again to see if it is the right length. It is always good when finishing off curtains to put lead weights in the hem as this makes them hang cleanly and sharply. A very wide, stiff Rufflette tape at the top of the curtains also gives a nice neat finish.

One can re-cover a faded, battered old Victorian chair or sofa quite easily by simply making a pattern out of old material or cheap calico to start with and pinning this on to the piece of furniture, wrong sides together. You literally cut the material on the sofa until it fits perfectly, pinning all the time, leaving about half an inch for seams. Then remove the cheap material and place this pattern on to the fabric of your choice, pinning it on and cutting very carefully around it. This way there is no wastage and you can therefore use much more expensive material than you thought you could afford – it still works out at about a tenth of the price of having it done professionally.

Where you can, do as many machine-stitched seams as possible. Simply place the fabric wrong side downwards on to the furniture and pin the two sides together. Then tack them, check for fit, machine stitch them together, and finally, of course, press the seams.

There are bound to be places where you cannot machine-stitch the fabric – for example when you have got as much of the cover on to the piece of furniture as you can and you've come to the awkward bits around the arms. With these you need to gather the material on to the arms and pin very carefully; you will then have to hand sew or, if that is not possible, stick with a fabric glue but always pin first. You can then cover the rough edge with matching or contrasting braid, which can also be glued. The same applies to wooden-framed furniture where you have to tack the fabric on. It is always best to turn the edge of the material over before tacking down, as this prevents it from fraying. Then, of course, you simply cover the tacks with braid, which is glued into place.

As with upholstery, very effective results can be achieved quite simply in home decorating. Try putting on three coats of emulsion, the first a matt base colour; then take one of those very large natural sea sponges and a pair of rubber gloves and sponge either a lighter or a darker colour over the base colour while the undercoat is still slightly wet. This creates a very dramatic, Baroque effect in a bedroom, for example. You can then highlight the whole by flinging the contents of a loaded brush full of gold or silver paint at the wall in an uninhibited manner. This produces a wonderfully dense, mottled effect, especially if done in very dark, romantic colours.

I always mix my own emulsion paints to achieve the colour I want. For some reason manufacturers don't seem to produce exactly the right shade for me. So, for example, I get the really dark green that I require by mixing a shop-bought dark green with black or very dark grey. The same applies to a dark red or plum. Do make a note of the quantities of each colour that you've used in your bespoke paint mixture, or you'll never be able to repeat it – a disaster if you run out of mixed paint in the middle of the room!

Wallpapering I find a different matter altogether – extremely difficult and fiddly. I have attempted it on several occasions with, I fear, only a limited amount of success – I prefer to leave it to the professionals. I once made some patchwork wallpaper. I cut out squares and rectangles from several different rolls of wallpaper that I had picked up in a remnant sale and pasted them on my bathroom walls like a patchwork quilt. It looked divine and original and I used to lie in the bath happily gazing at my efforts. (This last sentence could easily be misinterpreted, but I'm leaving it anyway.)

I have already touched on the 'hostess' side of domestic life, and explained that my belief in food-as-fuel, and my moral rejection of the idea of food-as-pleasure, does rather restrict my activities in this sphere. Being a pagan, I have always found Christmas rather tedious. I don't think I am alone in this sentiment: I understand that full-blooded Christians also find it a rather tiresome time of year. However, I do my best to enter into the spirit of the thing. This is all perfectly legitimate, for the feast of Christmas is simply a pagan celebration which has been taken over by the Christian Church for everyone's mutual convenience. It being much easier to adopt the existing feast days of the old religion and gently infiltrate the new ideas into the populace rather than completely revamp the entire proceedings. So at the feast of Yule I do not indulge in the usual Christmas fare or indeed in what is now regarded as conventional decoration. I go out and collect holly, mistletoe and ivy, tie them together and then string whole garlands of them across beams, along shelves or ledges and around the table.

Being a vegetarian as well as a pagan does rather place limitations on one's enjoyment of the festivities. My main meal at Christmas consists of Christmas pudding. I have Christmas pudding for the main course and Christmas pudding for pudding. This is followed by Christmas pudding for tea and Christmas pudding for the next few days, interspersed with the odd salad, parsnip or leek. But as you can get those things at other times of the year, the only seasonal celebratory indulgence for me is Christmas pudding. This is invariably accompanied by plain live yoghurt which counteracts the excessive sweetness of the pudding.

Having been brought up as a Roman Catholic I am a cynic in the true meaning of the word. That does not mean to say that I do not have my hedonistic side, but I believe the original philosophy of cynicism stated that the true meaning of life could only be realised by suffering a great deal. In other words life had to be painful to be appreciated fully and should not consist of the pursuit of pleasure, which I believe is what hedonism means. So, being of a rather cynical disposition, I always feel that I have to suffer in order to counter any excessive pleasure. The phrase 'once a Catholic' is indeed a true one; the morals and ethics one learns in one's formative years stick to one like a burr, and I have never been able to rid myself of the guilt that accompanies any form of indulgence or experience of pleasure. So the double cream and the home-made brandy butter are rejected in favour of the plain, simple rather bitter taste of live yoghurt; then all is well and I can enjoy myself – almost!

I am, as I have mentioned, a bit of a jam-maker. On one occasion when making jam for charity I produced an extraordinary concoction which I decided to call Frampold Jam. I was at the time appearing in *The Merry Wives of Windsor*; 'and the play contains the word 'frampold', an Elizabethan term now sadly out of common usage. It means difficult, and I have to say that this jam was some of the most difficult I have ever made. It simply refused to set, so I named it Frampold Jam. I often wonder what the people who bought it made of that particular name, and if they liked the contents. It was delicious by the time I had finished with it, but not conventional. I think that concoction from the O'Mara kitchen sums up my attitude to home-making, and perhaps to life in general. I won't be beaten by a situation, I'll invariably find a solution, it may well be a good one, it's usually unconventional and it's always uniquely me.

9

The Future Is The Rest Of My Life

O ne of the great things about life is that you never know what is going to happen next, what lies around the next corner. Even I, who have always prided myself on being ready for anything, have been caught amidships quite often. I am always faintly surprised when I find I have made it to another day, and haven't got run over by a bus or been involved in some ghastly car accident. But always supposing that I survive both these possibilities, I think I know what I would like the future to hold for me.

I do not wish to grow old gracefully. I do not want to settle down, or have peace or quiet. That would unnerve me completely – I simply would not know how to cope. I am all right so long as there is a really major drama going on in my life; that is

147

familiar terrain and I can play my manoeuvres accordingly. I see my life as a battlefield in which I am continually being forced to plan hasty campaigns and regroup my forces for an all-out attack. Not for me the stealthy approach. I don full warpaint and hurl myself upon the enemy shrieking blood-curdling war cries.

One thing I know for sure. I loathe being Kate O'Mara, this sort of raunchy sex symbol that has been created by the tabloid press. I have no idea who she is – she certainly isn't me. She is a part I have played, obviously very successfully, on popular television. And she has taken over quite a large chunk of my life, for which I resent her bitterly. It matters not a jot to anyone that I spend three-quarters of my life working in the theatre, mounting productions of the classics and appearing in them; touring the country in great drama both old and new; giving poetry recitals, lecturing on Shakespeare, and doing workshops on classical drama. To the popular press, and therefore the general public, I am simply a 'soap queen'. Nothing could be further from the truth, but what the hell can I do about it? If I deliberately destroyed my looks and figure and started playing character parts, I dare say the press would simply label me as an 'ex-soap queen'. Somewhere along the way something has gone terribly wrong.

Of course it is true that people have been to see me in Shakespeare plays who would not only not normally go to see Shakespeare but wouldn't even go to the theatre. They are always surprised that they have enjoyed themselves, they tell me, having been daunted by the very name 'Shakespeare' all their lives. So I suppose I have managed to do some good somewhere. I guess the die is cast and I just have to plough on as usual. What a ghastly mixed metaphor! However an agricultural analogy would, I think be appropriate here – something about land lying fallow and then reaping the harvest – but somehow chance has crept in unbidden as though I had no control over the matter.

THE FUTURE IS THE REST OF MY LIFE

What does it matter anyway? As I said before, the great thing about life and in particular the acting profession is that you never know what may happen next. I went to Hollywood at forty-six when I least expected it. Anything can happen. People often ask me how I feel about getting older. I always find that a very difficult question to answer, for the simple reason that I do not feel that I am getting older. I have the same amount of energy and enthusiasm and zest for life that I had at nineteen. Of course there are visible signs of physical ageing, but as they come gradually I have had time to get used to them and at the moment they do not worry me unduly. But I am sure they will in due course. I suppose then I shall become 'ageing ex-soap queen'. You just can't win.

I am not good at losing. All my life I have been a rebel, an outlaw; I hate to conform, and seldom have. I love breaking the rules. I have paid dearly for this and will doubtless continue to pay, but it is the only way that I know. I don't know how else to conduct my life. I am a creature of instinct and impulse. I have no plan, I improvise continually. I grab each situation by the throat and shake it into submission. I always 'go for it'.

I hope that I may be able to regard with equanimity whatever the future brings, regardless of whether I have to face it alone or with a male companion by my side. I think I would prefer the latter, simply because it stops one being too selfish. I am so into survival, almost at any cost, that I tend to forget about other people's needs. It is good to have someone else to worry about, care about and listen to. But even if this particular scenario does not materialise it would be nice to think that I can follow my own advice and survive alone.

One is never really alone, of course. I have countless friends to whom I am devoted. I am very fortunate in this respect. I also have a very loving, supportive family about whom I also care very deeply. They are all used to me battling on alone and I think regard my solitary campaign with amusement. At least I give

149

them a certain amount of entertainment. 'What new ghastly drama has O'Mara got herself into now?' I hear them cry from time to time. It is with great relish that I regale them with the latest adventure. They expect it to be pretty hot stuff and I hate to disappoint them. I love to shock, outrage, and above all entertain. I think I usually succeed.